The Great Equal Society

Confucianism, China and the 21st Century

The Great Equal Society

Confucianism, China and the 21st Century

Young-oak Kim

Hanshin University, Korea

Jung-kyu Kim

ACA Investments Pte Ltd, Singapore

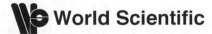

NEW JERSEY · LONDON · SINGAPORE · BEIJING · SHANGHAI · HONG KONG · TAIPEI · CHENNAI

Published by

World Scientific Publishing Co. Pte. Ltd.
5 Toh Tuck Link, Singapore 596224
USA office: 27 Warren Street, Suite 401-402, Hackensack, NJ 07601
UK office: 57 Shelton Street, Covent Garden, London WC2H 9HE

Library of Congress Cataloging-in-Publication Data
Kim, Yong-ok, 1948–
    The great equal society : Confucianism, China and the 21st century / Young-oak Kim,
Jung-kyu Kim.
        pages cm
    Includes bibliographical references and index.
    ISBN 978-9814504713 (softcover : alk. paper)
    1. Confucian sociology. 2. Confucianism. 3. China--Social conditions--21st century.
4. China--Economic conditions--21st century. 5. China--Politics and government--21st century.
I. Title.
    HN40.C6K57 2013
    306.0951--dc23

                                                    2013028181

British Library Cataloguing-in-Publication Data
A catalogue record for this book is available from the British Library.

In-house Editors: Zheng Danjun/Dong Lixi

Typeset by Stallion Press
Email: enquiries@stallionpress.com

Printed in Singapore

Acknowledgments

Let us be the first to acknowledge that this book borrows heavily from a dozen or so social science books which we have found particularly excellent and well-summarized. We don't mention them here because all external sources of information have been acknowledged meticulously throughout the book. As we have often relied on secondary sources for the latest findings in sociology, psychology, economics, and political science, there are instances where we have failed to credit original researchers for their contribution. We apologize to them, and encourage our readers to look up the sources in the endnotes if they want to read about the original work and draw their own conclusions. The only "original" insights we claim as our own lie in the interpretations of ancient Chinese texts, which sometimes diverge widely from conventional annotations, but even there we have only built on the pioneering work of sinologists who preceded us.

Contents

Preface

The concept of the Great Equal Society first appears in the *Book of Rites*, a Confucian classic which is said to have been compiled by Confucius. The description is as follows:

> When the Great Way prevails, public-mindedness rules all under Heaven. The worthy and the able are selected to office; their words are honest, and they cultivate harmony. Therefore, people don't just take care of their own parents, nor do they just favour their own children. The aged are cared for until the end of their lives, the able-bodied are properly employed, and the young are nurtured. Widows, widowers, orphans, the elderly, and the disabled are all cared for. Men have their proper work, while women have their homes. While people still value things, they don't just hoard things for themselves. While people still value their work, they don't just exert every effort for themselves. Selfishness is suppressed, and there are no thieves who filch or rebels who disrupt the society. So people don't lock their doors at night. This is called the Great Equal Society.[1]

This is the vision of Confucian utopia, which one may define as "a society where public-mindedness prevails over selfishness." The leadership is honest and competent. People have deeply ingrained habits of looking beyond their narrow self-interest. As such, the society is filled with mutual trust and goodwill, evidenced by the fact that people routinely leave their doors unlocked.

Unlike Christians, who believe Heaven is a place you reach only in the afterlife, Confucius thought his vision of utopia is attainable here on earth. And unlike Karl Marx, who believed the proletariat paradise would arrive overnight through a class war, Confucius maintained that the Great Equal Society could only be achieved gradually, through the right leadership and education. In modern times, the concept has inspired a generation of reformers in China, ranging from Kang You-wei, the political philosopher who tried (and almost succeeded in) bringing constitutional monarchy to China, to Dr. Sun Yat-sen, the "Father of the Nation" who ended millennia of imperial rule in China.

What happens when the Great Way breaks down, i.e. when people relentlessly pursue their self-interest at society's expense? The Master (Confucius) continues:

> When the Great Way falls into disuse and obscurity, familism rules all un-
> der the Heaven. People take care only of their own parents, and favour
> only their own children. People hoard wealth and exploit others' work...
> so-called leaders take their inherited privileges for granted, and they dig
> deep moats and build castle walls.[2]

The contrast with the Great Equal Society is striking. Once public trust breaks down, society becomes caught in a vicious cycle of mutual suspicion. People no longer trust strangers, until their circle of trust shrinks to their immediate family. Not only do people lock their doors, but the rulers rush to build stronger defences. Not only do individuals begin looking out only for themselves, but they have no qualms about exploiting others.

Unfortunately, it is this latter state which better describes China today. The country has achieved dazzling GDP growth but suffered a stunning collapse of social values along the way. The demise of communist ideals, combined with bold capitalist experiments, has left a materialistic culture which is breathtaking in its cynicism. How China may restore a society where mutual trust rather than suspicion prevails — in today's hyper-competitive world of global capitalism — is the primary theme of this book.

But then China is hardly alone in experiencing the "hollowing out" of public morality and the ensuing social ills. America, too, has undergone a steep decline in social cohesion, as demonstrated by its gated communities and bulging prisons. We find surprising similarities in the underlying social, political, and economical problems of East and West. Our goal is therefore not only to rejuvenate Confucianism for China but also to formulate a new social vision, based on a creative reinterpretation of Confucianism, to address the common problems which modernity poses for humanity.

* * *

We believe we are somewhat uniquely positioned to take on this admittedly ambitious assignment. The co-authors of this book, Young-oak and Jung-kyu, come from very different backgrounds. Young-oak has devoted his life to the study of philosophy. He steeped himself in the classics of both East and West. His knowledge of Christianity is just as deep as that of Buddhism, based as they are on decades of painstaking training in philology. He is one of the rare intellectuals who can easily leapfrog from a passage in *Tao Te Ching* to the process philosophy of Alfred North Whitehead. Jung-kyu, on the other hand, has a more pragmatic disposition. Even though he studied Chinese classics under Young-oak, he did not have the patience to stick with the world of academia. One of his favourite quotes at Harvard was one attributed to its star alumnus, Henry Kissinger: when a student asked why academic disputes are so bitter, Kissinger reportedly quipped, "Because the stakes are so low".[3] So, upon graduation, Jung-kyu eschewed the ivory tower and entered the "real world" of business.

We would like to think the nature of our collaboration resembles somewhat the relationship between Confucius and one of his disciples, Zigong. As an accomplished businessman and statesman, Zigong was concerned with practical rather than philosophical matters. He once confessed: "I was often able to hear the Master describe ordinary matters, but I was not able to hear the Master speak of the Nature of Man and the Ways of Heaven".[4] Confucius preferred not to discuss metaphysical subjects with a pragmatic man such as Zigong. But Zigong was a good student, who learned by always asking precise and tangible questions. Many of the best parts of the *Analects* are the exchanges between Confucius and Zigong, where Zigong forces concrete answers out of Confucius on familiar, everyday issues such as the priority of government, the nature of money, and even the management of friendship.[5]

The value Jung-kyu brings to this endeavor is similar. His acute interest in real-world issues facing his generation, such as rising inequality, rampant individualism, and environmental degradation, keeps this book grounded and relevant to our times, in instances where Young-oak the philosopher might veer in a more universal and abstract direction. This explains our unlikely teacher–student collaboration. The motivation driving this book is simple: we both want our society to be healthy and prosperous. The Great Equal Society is the concept we borrowed to symbolize this vision.

* * *

Because our subject matter straddles both East and West, all chapters share a somewhat unique structure. We begin each chapter by illustrating one of the key problems of a modern society, usually in the Western context. We then present the Confucian alternative, followed by the lessons it holds for China in the 21st century.

Chapter 1 lays out the main issue which this book aims to address, namely the retrenchment of social values in both East and West, and explains why a fundamental shift in philosophy is required to tackle this urgent and important problem.

The next triad of chapters discusses proposals for better government, economy, and education. Chapter 2 begins by asking whether democratic reforms are necessary for China. We then proceed to present the Confucian approach to governance, with a particular focus on addressing the issues of endemic corruption and crony capitalism. Chapter 3 explores why many businesspeople — mostly upright citizens in their private lives — act without scruples at work, and what we may do to mitigate the dehumanizing forces of market competition. We then put forward the Confucian principle for building a humane economy, with specific remedies proposed at state, corporate, and individual levels. In Chapter 4, we take a stab at perhaps the most intractable problem of all, namely how we may rein in the destructive competition for higher educational credentials — an arms race which shows no sign of abating while unduly burdening family finances everywhere.

In the final chapter, we review the main arguments of the book and explain how the "China model" should evolve going forward. We also address two topics which matter greatly to China's future and concern the rest of mankind, namely diplomacy and the environment, before wrapping up the book with our vision for the future of China. For those readers seeking a deeper understanding of Confucianism, we have also included a bonus chapter which explores its fundamentals in greater detail.

This book is a work of philosophy, a rare breed in today's publishing world. In it, we have laid out general principles as well as a functional blueprint for change, by leveraging the core insights of Confucianism and also by integrating and synthesizing the latest findings from various disciplines. It may strike some readers as strange that an ancient body of thought should inspire a book dealing with hyper-modern issues, but the fact of the matter is that, without attaching ourselves to a time-tested tradition, our arguments would lack the depth or authority which is required to supplant the prevailing mode of thought. As conservative columnist David Brooks once observed, "Applying an ancient tradition to a new situation is a creative, stimulating and empowering act".[6] This book is an exercise in "applying an ancient tradition to a new situation," and we hope our readers will find it as "creative, stimulating, and empowering" as we did.

Young-oak Kim and Jung-kyu Kim
February, 2013

1

A Philosophical Shift

The Master said, "A gentleman is enlightened by righteousness. A small man only understands profit."

Analects, 4-16

Johnson's Great Society

In his latest bestseller *11/22/63*, Stephen King speculates about what might have happened if John F. Kennedy had not been assassinated on that fateful November day. Would the world have changed for the better or for the worse? We do not want to give anything away, but one of the surprising possibilities King suggests is that without Kennedy's murder, the landmark civil rights bill may never have passed:

> The great civil rights reform of the sixties never happened. Kennedy was no LBJ, and as vice president, Johnson was uniquely powerless to help him. The Republicans and Dixiecrats filibustered for a hundred and ten days; one actually died on the floor and became a right-wing hero… The race riots came next.[1]

Although it is only conjecture, King could very well be correct in his assessment. According to Robert Caro, who recently published the fourth volume of his biography of Lyndon B. Johnson, the weeks following Kennedy's assassination turned out to be Johnson's "finest moment".[2] The former Senate leader rammed through the Civil Rights Act of 1964, taking advantage of his own legislative mastery and the outpouring of goodwill which understandably followed the tragedy. History often progresses in mysterious and unintended ways.

In spite of the circumstances that had brought him to power, Johnson seized the moment to enact his vision of the Great Society. The goal was not only to put an end to poverty and racial injustice but also to improve education, protect consumers, preserve the environment, and restore a sense of community. Here is how Johnson laid down the challenge in his historic address at the University of Michigan on May 22, 1964. (In another irony of history, standing next to him was George W. Romney, then governor of Michigan. He was a moderate Republican who strongly supported the Civil Rights Movement and fought hard to provide affordable housing for the poor. Mitt Romney is his youngest son.)

> For half a century we called upon unbounded invention and untiring industry to create an order of plenty for all of our people. The challenge of the next half century is whether we have the wisdom to use that wealth to enrich and elevate our national life, and to advance the quality of our American civilization… we have the opportunity to move not only toward the rich society and the powerful society, but upward to the Great Society.[3]

The landslide victory in 1964 gave Johnson the popular mandate — and a highly supportive Congress, with Democrats controlling more than two-thirds of each chamber — to implement his ambitious agenda. Without delving into the details, his major legislative achievements include: the Civil Rights Act (desegregation); the Social Security Act (Medicare and Medicaid); the Economic Opportunity Act (Job Corps); the Elementary and Secondary Education Act (Head Start); the Motor Vehicle Safety Act; the Public Broadcasting Act; and the National Environment Policy Act. While the legacy of Johnson's War on Poverty remains disputed, one telling statistic is that the percentage of Americans living below the poverty line dropped from 22.2% in 1963 to 12.6% in 1970. In particular, the proportion of African-Americans living in poverty declined from 55% to 27% around this period.[4]

When we translated the Chinese term *datong* as the Great Equal Society (rather than the Great Unity, as it is commonly rendered), it was partly meant as a tribute to Johnson's Great Society. Therefore, it is particularly distressing for us to point out that the achievements of the Great Society were gradually reversed in important ways over the subsequent decades. America today is more unequal than it was during the 1960s.[5] The education gap, which had been closing at one point, continues to widen relentlessly. About 50 million Americans, including 7 million children, do not have health insurance.[6]

On a more general level, the American political scene today is characterized by bitter partisanship, with brazen lies masquerading as election strategy, while the great majority of its businesses are engaged in the single-minded pursuit of profit, seemingly oblivious to all other human, social, and environmental considerations. If the ultimate goal of the Great Society was to "elevate our national life" and "advance the quality of our American civilization," then it clearly failed. In the political realm, we have a major political party which apparently decided its only goal was to win the next election — and wilfully triggered a budget crisis toward that end. In the economic realm, we have a whole sector which, in its short-sighted greed, precipitated the worst financial crisis since the Great Depression.

What this sad state of affairs shows is the limits of purely institution-based reform. The failure of the Great Society was not due to the lack of well-intentioned legislative efforts, but due to the culture of greed and selfishness which somehow pervaded all levels of American society. How could the American elite ever allow this to happen? In our opinion, the main culprit was the widely held belief that the pursuit of self-interest was the "rational" thing to do. Any other mode of behavior — say, a cab driver charging less fare to a blind woman, a phenomenon which is surprisingly common — was considered "irrational" and demanded explanation based on selfish reasons (e.g. "ego motivation," meaning the cab driver just wanted to feel good about himself).[7] Not only was the utilitarian calculation of self-interest condoned as the "natural" thing to do, but it was actively encouraged as the "right" thing to do — a philosophical stance known as rational egoism, coined by

Ayn Rand in *The Virtue of Selfishness*. When we pursue this line of thinking to its logical extreme, we arrive at Gordon Gekko's famous dictum in the film *Wall Street*: "Greed is good." It was this kind of unquestioning belief in rational self-interest which slowly tore apart the fabric of Protestant morality, which had once upheld this great nation.

Restoring Inner Morality

So what is to be done? We felt the answer would not be found within the Enlightenment tradition of the West, because the entire edifice of the Enlightenment, also known as the Age of Reason, lies on the bedrock of rational self-interest — and the negative view of human nature it necessarily entails. Rational self-interest, which currently serves as the standard postulate of human behavior in our political, economic, and social sciences, is a barren and sad view of human nature. It assumes that everyone in society is functioning only to maximize his self-interest. If we follow this view, a human being is essentially reduced to a machine (which only calculates) or a beast (which only follows its libido).[8] Democracy and capitalism merely become mechanisms by which competing interests — clashing libidos, if you will — are somehow sorted out without resorting to an all-out war. But is that all there is to human nature?

For a truly alternative perspective, we have turned to our own tradition in the East, namely Confucianism. Confucius held that the most essential attribute of a human being is not the profit motive but *ren*. What is *ren*? While *ren* is commonly translated as "benevolence," the term originally meant "an ability to feel" or "empathy" — an ability to imagine oneself in another's shoes — and its meaning has later expanded to include new connotations such as compassion, aesthetic sensibility, and humaneness. Confucius thought it constituted the basis of morality, suggesting that those who possess *ren* — those who can truly feel — cannot help but be moral. Mencius took this line of thinking further to assert that we are all born with a moral inclination, and that our innate moral impulse is at least as strong as our desire for money or sex. Is this not a much richer, and more realistic, view of human nature, one which treats mankind with proper dignity and respect? A millennium later, Neo-Confucians argued that by cultivating one's moral nature — and by exercising it toward the betterment of society at large — anyone could aspire to achieve "sagehood": self-cultivation and social realization were seen as the keys to leading a meaningful and satisfactory life. Why does one feel more comfortable and fulfilled when he follows *ren*, cultivates himself, and devotes himself to his family and society? It is because human beings are aesthetic, perfectible, and social by nature.

We see here that morality for Confucians is not about following a set of rigid rules based on God's decrees; rather, it involves the active choice of a virtuous life based on an enlightened understanding of human nature. Confucians sought to promote a moral society through persuasion and examples — awakening the goodness within, if you will — rather than through incentives and punishments. In fact, one might argue that moral acts achieved via carrots and sticks are not really moral at all, if one defines morality as "doing the right thing when no one else is watching." Imagine a classroom full of students. When the class ends, students pile out of the room. There is a piece of trash on the way out. Most students ignore it, but one student decides to pick it up. What is special about his act? For the student in question, there is no material incentive to be gained, or physical punishment to be avoided, by taking care of the trash. To borrow Kant's distinction, he is just following his categorical imperative (doing something because the thing is good in itself) rather than a hypothetical imperative (doing the right thing on the condition that it leads to a reward later). This seemingly trivial example illustrates perfectly the essence of what we mean by inner morality.

The Great Equal Society, which we defined as "a society where public-mindedness prevails over selfishness," is nothing other than a society where its members *autonomously* do the right thing. Such a society can do without overly complicated rules, because one trusts that most people will act decently most of the time. To be sure, some kind of law enforcement is required to keep the society in order, but it is only called upon as a means of last resort — that is, after efforts at edification have failed. Paradoxically, such a society is actually *freer* than a society which prizes individual liberty above all else. Let us take America again as a counterexample. Although Americans cherish their ideal of untrammelled freedom, America has increasingly become a police state where one constantly feels watched, crimped, and corralled.[9] We (the authors) feel fearful when we encounter a law enforcement officer in New York, in a way we never would in front of a policeman in Tokyo. What with all the litigation and security cameras, we do not see how Americans consider themselves the freest people in the world. Compare such a society with the Great Equal Society where "people don't lock doors at night." Which would you rather live in — a society where you have to be ever vigilant, or one where you can let your guard down and relax?

If a society as a whole valued and practiced the virtue of *ren*, then members of such a society would be filled with benevolence and goodwill toward one another. Confucius captured this utopian ideal with a powerful image: a society without lawsuits.

> The Master said, "When it comes to hearing and adjudicating a legal dispute, I can be as good as anybody. But what I really want is this: to govern in such a way that people do not need to sue one another!"[10]

For Confucius, widespread litigation was the symbol of mistrust and contention which characterized a money-grabbing society. Instead of spending a fortune on armies of lawyers and thick contracts, should we not restore humanity and morality to our society, so that we do not have to sue one another? A society without lawsuits is a society where the spirit of cooperation prevails over narrow self-interest; this, in turn, is the very definition of the Great Equal Society.

Institution versus Culture

How does the ancient vision of the Great Equal Society, with its emphasis on inner morality, relate to contemporary issues facing China?

Many people assume China can become a responsible world power only through a radical change in its political system. It is not just outsiders who think this way. For example, Jiang Qing (not the last wife of Chairman Mao but the influential author of *Political Confucianism*) proposes that China adopt a tricameral legislature, consisting of three houses: people's representatives chosen by popular election, Confucian elites chosen by competitive examination, and elites entrusted with the task of cultural continuity (a Chinese version of the British House of Lords).[11]

Surely, a lot of careful thought has gone into building this kind of proposal, but we find such discussion a bit hollow. For one thing, the political system in China is hardly broken: the Chinese Communist Party (henceforth referred to as "the party") has already managed three consecutive transitions of power in a peaceful and orderly manner, and it continues to produce capable technocrats based on its well-defined merit system, correction system, and learning system. Unlike politicians in the West, who waste much of their time preparing for the next election, the mandarins in Beijing can concentrate their resources on long-term planning and execution of vital policies. We will examine this issue more deeply in the following chapter, but for now, let us stress that the party is here to stay, given the unique history of modern China and the legitimacy the party has acquired over the years.

The more fundamental problem with Jiang Qing's approach is that he appears too obsessed with building the right *system*. We are not suggesting a system is not important. A democratic system allows voters to kick out incompetent leaders. A capitalist system allows consumers to weed out (by voting with their wallets) incompetent corporations. The beauty of both the democratic system and the capitalist system is that, to a certain extent, the system can be agnostic about the *character* of the individuals who operate it. Rational voters and consumers, out of self-interest, automatically ensure that the best leaders and corporations survive competition. Theoretically at least, it doesn't matter whether the individual leaders or corporations are moral or not. As Adam Smith famously observed in *The Wealth of Nations*, "It is not from the benevolence of the butcher, the brewer, or the baker that we expect our dinner, but from their regard to their own interest." Why rely on the kindness or humanity of others, when their self-seeking and greed will do the job?

Because, in the real world, self-interest alone will *not* do the job. Inner morality — doing the right thing when no one else is watching — matters, in almost every walk of our lives. What ails China is not the lack of elective democracy or free enterprise. It is what we read about in newspapers everyday — corrupt bureaucrats and unethical businessmen, for example. Underlying these problems is a fundamental deficit of social values.

Horror stories of unsafe food made in China abound, ranging from fish contaminated with banned drugs to toothpaste and cough syrup made with toxic chemicals to lead paint used on toys.[12] More than 145 patients were killed in Panama from Chinese cough medicine in 2006, the same year that scores fell ill and six died from a contaminated antibiotic in China. Two years before that, a dozen babies died from infant formula of little nutritional value in what is known as the "big-headed babies" scandal. The most high-profile case to date may be that of Sanlu, which had long been the top producer of infant formula in China. Then, shortly after the Olympics, news surfaced that its milk was contaminated with melamine, a nitrogen-rich chemical commonly used to make plastic and fertilizer. China's health ministry estimated that 300,000 babies had been taken ill due to contaminated milk powder. This came on the heels of the melamine-contaminated pet food scandal the previous year, when hundreds of dogs and cats had died in the US due to ingredients imported from China.

What do these sad stories tell us? Morality of the participants matters, even under the supposedly self-correcting capitalist system. If all we had was self-interest, this modern society of ours would fall apart any minute. Arthur Miller, an American playwright, describes in a 1947 play *All My Sons* (based on a true story) a father who supplies defective aircraft parts which cause planes to crash. Eventually his son, choosing his conscience over filial loyalty, reports his father. There were moments, Miller wrote, "when an individual conscience was all that could keep a world from falling".[13] He seemed to understand how precarious and valuable the prosperity of his society was, supported as it was by the inner morality of millions of individuals who quietly and dutifully toiled at their jobs. As Cambridge economist Ha-Joon Chang puts it, "[I]f the world were full of the self-seeking individuals found in economics textbooks, it would grind to a halt... The world works as it does only because people are not the totally self-seeking agents that free-market economics believes them to be".[14] This is why we believe the primary challenge for China is not institutional but cultural: how to revive its social values and restore morality, so that its bureaucrats may become less corrupt, and its merchants more honest.

Just to be clear, institutional safeguards also matter. Possibly the greatest failure of Confucianism was that due to its emphasis on "rule by men" over "rule by law," it never gave birth to the notion of constitutional rights, or other forms of checks on absolutist power, as the West did. What we are saying, though, is that we should shift our focus from institution-building to instilling civic virtue and cultivating moral leadership — and this is a lesson which applies equally to America as it does to China. Barring such a cultural transformation, purely institution-driven reform is bound to flounder, as the aforementioned failure of Johnson's Great Society demonstrates. And vice versa: for the most graphic illustration of why having the right institution matters, just think of the astonishing disparity between North Korea and South Korea, two countries which largely share the same geography, history, and culture.[15] At the risk of oversimplification, we may summarize by saying that the key task of China in the 21st century will be leveraging the strengths of the West (institution) to supplement those of its own tradition (culture).

A Society of *Ren*: Modern Examples

We have defined the Great Equal Society as a society where public-mindedness prevails over selfishness. Its members can be counted on to autonomously do the right thing, as they have deeply ingrained habits of looking beyond their narrow self-interest. Confucius illustrated his vision with such powerful imageries as "a society without lawsuits" and a place where "people don't lock their doors at night." They all sound wonderful, but what would such a society actually look like in today's world?

Clues can be found in the "post-Confucian" societies of Asia, such as Japan, Korea, Taiwan, and Singapore. As it turns out, Japan is as close to "a society without lawsuits" as a modern capitalist society can get. Legal agreements rarely run longer than two pages. When it comes to establishing confidence between two parties, the informal cues — presenting a name card with two hands and bowing respectfully, for example — matter as much as the legalistic ones. As *The Economist* observes on the Japanese business culture:

> Business disputes rarely go to trial. The number of corporate lawyers is extremely low compared with other financial centres, and frauds by one party against another are exceedingly rare.[16]

Is there a lesson to be learned here? We have mentioned that Confucius regarded rampant litigation as a symbol of mistrust and contention which characterize a money-grabbing society. What distinguishes Japan from the legalistic societies of the West is its Confucian culture which values social harmony and contribution to community over selfishness. As Francis Fukuyama points out in his book *Trust*, capitalism works best when its individualism is moderated by public spirit.[17]

Oftentimes, what truly impress visitors to Japan is not its high-tech gadgets, impeccable fashion, or first-rate cuisine; rather, it is the simple decency of its people, as shown by their courtesy and hospitality. American sports writers got a taste of it during the 1998 Winter Olympics in Nagano. For example, Dave Barry of the *Miami Herald* noted three paradoxes of Japan: first, "[t]he police are unarmed, but everybody obeys the law"; second, "[y]ou almost never see trash cans, but you never see litter, either"; third, "[t]here is no tipping, but the service is fantastic".[18] The reason Barry finds them perplexing is because there is absolutely no link between material incentives (carrots and sticks) and actions being performed. In fact, there is no mystery at all: all three "paradoxes" are simply instances of *inner morality* at work, defined as doing the right thing even if no one else is watching.

In another example, George Vecsey of *The New York Times* documented the testimony of Gold medal winning female hockey players of the US as well as his own reaction in a column titled "A Verbal Gold Medal to a Perfect Host Nation":

> "I left my phone in the van," said Angela Ruggiero, [a US] hockey player. "I got back to the village and called the number on my phone, and the driver of the van answered. He didn't speak a word of English and I don't speak Japanese, but I got somebody in the village to speak to him in Japanese and somehow they got the phone back to me."
>
> Everybody has a story like that: the volunteer who drove in the snow to find a missing telephone cable. The bus driver who made an unscheduled stop to let a few people out near their destination. The people in the cafeteria who struggled to understand my phrase-book mumblings that I did not want meat in my noodles. They were not here for an interesting Olympic experience. They were here to serve.[19]

During our time in Japan, we (the authors) were constantly struck by how genuine this desire "to serve" is. Suppose you ask a young girl what she wants to be when she grows up, and she replies, say, "A nurse." You ask her why. She will tell you it is because she wants to be "useful" to other people (*yaku ni tachitai*). Compare this attitude with what children are being taught in a more individualistic culture, where the key lesson might as well be "not being used" by others. The former attitude exemplifies a fundamentally benign worldview, which assumes the best about one another's intentions; the latter, a hostile worldview, which assumes everyone is out to take advantage of one another. Which world would you rather live in? To put it another way, we may say the Japanese culture is characterized by a profound sense of *gratitude*. Because one is deeply grateful for what others in his society have done for him, he is eager to play his part by being socially responsible. Nothing kindles one's innate goodness like a random act of kindness by a stranger. A more individualistic culture, on the other hand, exhibits a strong sense of *entitlement*, often tinged with bitterness at not being given what one is justly entitled to. Our satisfaction in life depends a great deal on which attitude we choose to adopt.

All this is not to deny that Japan has its share of problems. What ails Japan is the opposite of what we are trying to address in this book, in the sense that its problems are primarily institutional rather than cultural. Although Japan's elite tends to be relatively able and selfless, the decision-making authority is so dispersed that it is nearly impossible for any individual leader to overrule minority objection in a top-down fashion. Such a consensus-driven system has the benefit of being inclusive and egalitarian, but it can also lead to the groupthink and paralysis which are so characteristic of Japanese politics.

Nonetheless, we have dwelled upon the Japanese example in some length, because it goes to the heart of our agenda in writing this book: to build a kind and gentle society, where mutual trust and civic-mindedness, rather than suspicion and selfishness, prevail. Such traits are by no means limited to Japan. In fact, America during its halcyon days was also notable for its widely shared values and vibrant culture of civic engagement. As Charles Murray, a conservative academic, wistfully notes:

> By 1963, crime had been low for many years. In large swathes of America, doors were routinely left unlocked, children were allowed to move around the neighbourhood unsupervised, and, except in the toughest neighbourhoods of the largest cities, it seldom occurred to someone walking alone at night to worry about muggers.[20]

If we define the Great Equal Society as a place where "people don't lock their doors at night," America during the early sixties would definitely fit the description. But then something went wrong. America today, with its gated communities and bulging prisons, would hardly qualify as a Great Equal Society. The decline in social cohesion was not due to some external economic shock such as globalization and IT. Nor does the blame lie with liberation of women, minorities, and homosexuals, as some right-wing commentators claim.[21] As we have argued, the real culprit is an unquestioning belief in rational self-interest, which gradually pervaded our classrooms, boardrooms, and policy caucuses. Ironically, what our diagnosis implies is that the decline *can* be reversed, as the underlying cause is primarily philosophical. For that to happen, though, we must recognize that selfishness (even of the enlightened sort) is ultimately a poor basis for morality and introduce a new philosophy based on the values of compassion, aesthetic sensibility, and humaneness (*ren*) instead.

A New Philosophy for China — and for the World

Philosophy matters. Although it is hard to imagine today, philosophy used to be the king of all sciences. Then, starting around the 18th century, sciences began to crystallize and subdivide, and the "natural philosophers," as opposed to moral and mathematical philosophers, began calling themselves "scientists" instead.[22] What remained of philosophy has further branched out, and the offshoots have formed many of the academic disciplines we know today: mathematics, linguistics, political science, jurisprudence, sociology, economics, and psychology, just to name a few. Having shed the natural and social sciences, academic philosophy nowadays can feel like an empty shell, devoid of content and irrelevant to the real world. Some people liken modern philosophy to King Lear, an impotent old man who wanders aimlessly after giving away all his territories to his children.

As we purport to demonstrate in this book, however, philosophical assumptions shape our society in non-obvious but profound ways. Specifically, the assumption of rational self-interest, which currently dominates our political, economic, and social discourse, has bred a culture of extreme individualism and profit-seeking, which is undermining our social relationships and moral values.

In the US, the public is aggrieved and enraged, seeing the Wall Street investment bankers who caused the financial crisis revel in record profits and huge bonuses, while the taxpayers who paid for the bailout suffer the prospect of layoffs and foreclosures. Unfortunately, their legitimate indignation often expresses itself in the form of the Tea Party Movement and other misguided activisms.

As Noam Chomsky, a leading public intellectual in the US, laments:

> People rightly want answers, and they are not getting them except from voices that tell tales that have some internal coherence — if you suspend disbelief and enter into their world of irrationality and deceit.[23]

In the absence of genuine philosophical alternatives, many people have chosen the "ecstatic escape of unreason" by committing themselves to radical ideologies and religions.[24] What is the difference between philosophy on the one hand, and ideology and religion on the other? While philosophy seeks to illuminate reality through open-minded discussion and clarification, ideology and religion tend to impose dogmatic beliefs and shun criticism. What we need today is a real philosophy to help us make sense of the world, not a bunch of "-isms" telling us what to believe.

Nowhere is the need for philosophy more apparent than in China, a country which has been overtaken by materialist values in recent years. How did this happen? A turning point may have been the Tiananmen Square protests of 1989. University students who organized the protests were a highly idealistic lot, who genuinely believed that China could become a better (not just richer) society through further liberalization and reform. They drew inspiration from the free societies of the West, as demonstrated by the makeshift replica of the Statue of Liberty, erected during the final days of the protests. The Chinese Communist Party tried to appease them at first, but when the movement threatened to get out of hand, Deng Xiaoping ordered in tanks to squash it.

The tragedy here is that Deng was seen by most students as something of a hero in those days. For them, it was Deng who had the courage to confront Mao's loyalists during the fateful party assembly in December 1978, thereby setting China on a new course. It was Deng's two lieutenants, Zhao Ziyang and Hu Yaobang, who fought off hardliners within the party and advanced both economic and political reforms. Hu later paid the price for pushing on the political front too far, as he was removed from the post of general secretary in 1987, and it was his sudden death in April 1989 which triggered the Tiananmen Square protests. Still, it is not unreasonable to assume that most protesters would have regarded Deng's rule as fundamentally benign back then — and were hopeful their voices would eventually be heard by the party leadership. Imagine their disillusionment when the tanks rolled in and the massacre began!

What the students failed to understand was that Deng never had any coherent ideology, be it Marxism or liberalism. If anything, what guided him all along was his intense pragmatism, encapsulated in his unforgettable dictum: "It does not matter if it is a yellow cat or a black cat, as long as it catches mice." As Michael Schuman notes in his account of Deng's life, "When Deng spoke of democracy — which he did repeatedly — he did not mean the democracy of Lincoln... [but the students] were misled by Deng's talk of democracy".[25] Ever so pragmatic, Deng decided multiparty elections would be too chaotic for China, and he called in the army to restore order. His judgment that an open economy could co-exist with a closed political system turned out to be shrewd, as the Chinese economy continued to expand at a rapid clip. In the process, however, Deng drove a devil's bargain with the Chinese people: the party would deliver material well-being to the people, as long as they never again asked for political reform. The people duly acquiesced, intoxicated by the unprecedented wealth descending upon them. The idealism of the student protesters was replaced by cynical pragmatism and money worship. As Mark Kitto, an old China hand, observes in a recent column:

> Modern day mainland Chinese society is focused on one object: money and the acquisition thereof... Traditional family culture... has become a "me" culture. Except where there is economic benefit to be had, communities do not act together... Social status, so important in Chinese culture... is defined by the display of wealth. Cars, apartments, personal jewellery, clothing, pets: all must be new and shiny, and carry a famous foreign brand name. In the small rural village where we live I am not asked about my health or that of my family, I am asked how much money our small business is making, how much our car cost, our dog.[26]

The party effectively offered bread as a substitute for freedom. With their hopes for a just society thwarted, the Chinese people had no choice but to accept it. We are not suggesting that the party should have given in to the protesters and adopted Western-style democracy. Under the circumstances, Deng made a reasonable choice. What we are saying, though, is that the death of lofty idealism, combined with

the policy of "growth at all costs," has gradually led to the retrenchment of social values. The "Confucian" culture we observe in China
today is a very corrupt form of Confucianism, which can best be
described as a toxic mixture of selfish familism and authoritarianism.

Just as in the US, what is desperately needed in China right now
is a real philosophy which provides answers to its most urgent social
problems, such as rising inequality and rampant individualism;
explains why things most people value currently are not the things
that should be valued; shows why it matters to lead one's life the right
way, however discouraging circumstances may be; and helps people
envision an alternate reality which they can collectively bring about.[27]
A fundamental shift in philosophy is the only way the Chinese society
as a whole can revive its aspiration of building a just and fair society.

Chapter

2

On Government

Lord Chi asked Confucius, "I am worried about thieves in the state. How do
I bring them under control?" Confucius replied, "If your Highness were not
greedy, people would not steal, even if you rewarded them for doing so."

Analects, 12-18

Is Democracy for China?

At the moment, a sense of helplessness prevails among electorates in
the West. It feels as though the democratic system of government,
which served them so well in the past, has largely stopped functioning. In America, deep division between the two major parties is
nothing new, but what we have witnessed lately is a kind of
hyper-partisanship which makes the job of governing all but
impossible. The debt ceiling crisis in August 2011, which nearly
brought the government to a standstill, is still fresh in our memory.
Due to the resulting paralysis, America suffered the humiliation of a
downgrade in its credit rating for the first time in history. Even more
disturbing is the ongoing failure of the federal government to
seriously address any of the nation's long-term challenges, such as its
ballooning deficit, decrepit infrastructure, deteriorating public
schools, rising income inequality, and lack of an energy-environment
strategy.

Now imagine you are Chinese. Outsiders keep telling you that China must adopt a Western-style democracy. How would you react? A naïve US senator (John McCain) recently warned China's vice foreign minister that "the Arab Spring is coming to China".[1] We can easily imagine the vice foreign minister rolling his eyes. Unlike some democracies of the West, China has a well-functioning and effective government. Its infrastructure development is the most obvious example. While Americans routinely endure crumbling roads, unsafe bridges, and aging airports, China has been erecting one impressive infrastructure after another with breathtaking efficiency. Thomas Friedman, who co-authored *That Used To Be Us* with Michael Mandelbaum, cites the example of a massive new convention centre in Tianjin he recently visited, the construction of which took only eight months. He contrasts it with the broken subway escalators in his hometown in Maryland, which lay neglected for nearly six months. If "getting things done" is the sign of a good government, then the Chinese government is surely as good as any.

The macroeconomic steering by the Chinese government has also been superb, with the country posting three decades of rapid, uninterrupted growth. Perhaps the best symbol of China's growing economic clout is its currency. The renminbi is expected to replace the US dollar as the world's reserve currency around 2020, just as the US dollar supplanted the pound sterling in the early 20th century.[2] Over the last decade, the US dollar has lost over a quarter of its value against other major currencies, while the euro is struggling for survival. The renminbi, on the other hand, has been getting ever stronger, even with currency control in place.

Given the situation, it is hard to see why the West should be preaching to China about its political system and not the other way around. In some ways, the lack of popular election works to China's advantage. In America, endless election cycles mean that politicians are bound to spend the majority of their time campaigning rather than governing. Besides demanding too much of a politician's time, a more critical consequence of electioneering is that politicians of all stripes get beholden to special interests who contribute to their campaigns. Senator Evan Bayh of Indiana, who spoke to Friedman and Mandelbaum, describes the situation in stark terms:

> [The donors tell the candidates] 'We love you. You've been a good friend... So here's a list of our top ten issues. Why don't you go study that, fill it out, and give it back to us, because we'd love to help you out.' And these are going to be real votes on specific pieces of legislation!... It's about as close to corruption as you can come without actually crossing the line.[3]

The rising influence of money in American politics is captured in the term "corporatocracy" — an unholy alliance between business elites and Washington politicians — which doles out tax cuts to the wealthy, deregulation to polluting industries, and sweetheart contracts to government suppliers. American economist Jeffrey Sachs lists four major policy failures which arose from this nefarious alignment: mammoth defence spending (5% of GDP, larger than the sum of *all* discretionary government spending) which feeds the notorious military-industrial complex; reckless deregulation and the subsequent bailout of the financial services industry, which was largely driven by Wall Street; a stalemate over an energy-environment policy, which protects Big Oil; and skyrocketing healthcare costs (a mind-boggling 17% of GDP), which mainly benefit big pharmaceutical companies and private healthcare providers.[4]

Does China want any of this? We hope not. The advantage of the Chinese system is that because there is no next election to worry about, the mandarins in Beijing can focus their energy on long-term planning and the execution of vital policies. And they actually have time to meet with experts and study complicated policy issues. One particular feature of the Chinese system we admire is the Central Party School, which trains newly appointed high-ranking officials and retrains the old ones. According to *People's Daily*, it invites the best scholars from diverse disciplines to familiarize key officials, most of whom have engineering backgrounds, with the latest "Western political theory, economics, and frontier issues of contemporary law, religion, military affairs, science and technology".[5] The importance the party attaches to the education of its cadres is demonstrated by the fact that the last president of the school was Xi Jinping, China's new leader.

We are not suggesting that the West emulate the China model. As we shall see shortly, the party dictatorship is far from perfect. We do believe, however, that supposed superiority of Western-style democracy is overblown. It is time outsiders stopped prescribing democracy for China (although they can and should challenge China on specific policy failures, such as its abuse of human rights and continued oppression of Tibet). If the purpose of a democratic system is to ensure periodic change in leadership, China has been doing it peacefully for decades. While China may not hold popular elections, it does have a well-defined, rational mechanism for promoting officials internally. According to reports, Xi was designated the next general secretary because he had received the highest number of votes in a secret intraparty poll among grassroots and senior cadres.[6] Within the party, there are two predominant factions: the "populists," who want to ameliorate the growing income gap, and the "elitists," who favor a more free-market approach. Sounds a bit like the Democrats and the Republicans, doesn't it? Xi was chosen over Li Keqiang, a populist who was known as Hu Jintao's protégé, largely because Xi was seen as sufficiently neutral by both factions.[7] Is this consensus-based approach so different from, say, the way Yoshihiko Noda was chosen to succeed Naoto Kan as prime minister by the Democratic Party of Japan around the same period?

Xi is not a dictator along the line of Putin, Mubarak, or Kim Jong-il. He simply chairs the seven-member Standing Committee of the Politburo, which runs China by consensus. The agenda for him to carry out is already laid out in the party's latest five-year plan. China saw what happens when too much power is concentrated in one individual during the days of Chairman Mao, and it will not suffer such horror again.

One might ask: what about the democratic aspirations of the Chinese people, which we read so much about? Some Western observers, bent on seeing the Communist Party unseated from power by its own people, have pointed to thousands of "mass incidents" in the countryside. Although mass protests against corrupt local officials are common in the poverty-stricken interior — recently an open revolt in the southern village of Wukan grabbed international headlines — opinion polls consistently show that the Chinese have, in fact, a high level of trust in their central leadership. As *The Economist* observes, "Many ordinary Chinese are contemptuous of local authorities, but still believe that leaders in Beijing are benign".[8] Perhaps what the Chinese really want is not so much political reform *per se* as less corruption in the ranks of their civil servants.

Real Challenge for China

The real challenge facing China is cultural rather than institutional. As far as the party is concerned, the rampant culture of corruption is the single biggest threat to its survival — an enemy within, if you will. Just how bad are things? If we told you that China ranked 75th out of 183 countries in Transparency International's annual Corruption Perceptions Index, just behind Brazil and not far from Italy, it would probably not tell you much.[9] For more revealing episodes, let us turn to Richard McGregor's incomparable account in his book *The Party*.

When a former vice-mayor of Beijing was arrested shortly after the Olympics for taking bribes worth $1 million, many Chinese reacted not with horror but with genuine surprise that the sum was so small. After all, the vice-mayor had been entrusted with a billion-dollar construction budget in the run-up to the games. So he must have been one of the less greedy officials. One blogger even wrote, "He should count as a clean official. No need for a trial. Release him now!"[10] McGregor compares this episode with several other cases which surfaced in 2009: a railways bureau chief in Xinjiang, convicted of embezzling $3.6 million; a mid-level official in Shanghai, forced to divest assets worth $6 million; a party secretary in Sichuan, executed for taking $2.5 million; a local police chief in Guangdong, discovered with $4.4 million cash in his house; and a vice-mayor of Suzhou, sentenced for pocketing a staggering $12 million.[11] And these are just the tip of the iceberg, because anti-corruption investigations are often half-hearted, especially when they might implicate truly powerful people. As one official testifies off-record, "Anti-corruption work cannot be done thoroughly, because more than just a few people are involved".[12] Those who are caught get caught because they have been particularly egregious, unlucky, or both. By "unlucky" we mean that prosecution could take place for political reasons.

One gripping account involves an official named Ma De. When he first became vice-mayor of a prefecture-level city, he was determined to maintain his integrity. He turned off lights at night, because he did not want to deal with gift-bearers who would queue up outside his house. Then his colleagues began chiding him for his holier-than-thou behavior:

> If you do not accept the things which are brought to your doorstep, those people will think that you do not trust them. Are you pushing them into the arms of the other people? See how other people eat, drink and take massages. If you are going to become a lone commander, how can you do your work? If you do not accept the gifts, Ma De's regime will not be stable.[13]

Ma became unpopular among party cadres, and lost his job after a vote at the people's congress. After spending a decade in painful retrenchment, he at last learned the lesson and secured a party secretary job in another city by paying $100,000 in bribes. (This kind of "pay-to-play," or buying and selling of positions, is not uncommon in China.) This time, he thrived under the corrupt system, exploiting his position without scruples. By the time he was arrested in 2002, his family bank account had accumulated 20 million *yuan* (about $2.3 million at the time) in just under three years. The lesson of this sad tale is that the prevalent culture of profiteering, along with peer pressure, acts as a strong incentive for corruption. Once "moderate" corruption becomes an accepted social norm, people within the system will inevitably be susceptible to its influence.

Nowadays, the crooked officials are mockingly referred to as the "black-collar" class — so called because they wear black designer suits and drive black luxury cars, often flouting traffic laws.[14] They are the new elite of the Chinese society, smug in their power, status, and money. Do they feel the resentment of an angry mob under their feet? We are not sure they do. The arrogance of some party officials, especially the privileged "princelings" of senior party leaders, brings to mind a passage from the 1987 novel *Bonfire of the Vanities*, where Sherman McCoy, a self-regarded "Master of the Universe," looks down upon the cityscape of Manhattan:

> There it was, the Rome, the Paris, the London of the twentieth century, the city of ambition, the dense magnetic rock, the irresistible destination of all those who insist on being where things are happening — and he was among the victors! He lived on Park Avenue, the street of dreams! He worked on Wall Street, fifty floors up, for the legendary Pierce & Pierce, overlooking the world!... He was of that breed whose natural destiny it was... to have what they wanted![15]

Masters of the universe these days may live in Shanghai's Pudong or Beijing's Central Business District, but the intoxicating effect of money and status remains the same. Just as Wall Street turned many bright-eyed young grads into bloodsuckers chanting "Greed is good," we fear the Chinese Communist Party is breeding a culture of excessive pursuit of power and profit. For Chinese officials caught up in the rat race for promotion, it is either getting ahead at all costs (if you are on the fast track) or getting rich at all costs (if you are not on the fast track, you might as well concentrate on milking your current position).[16] In the midst of hyper-competition, what is missing is any sense of idealism or purpose. Just as Wall Street banks remain the most popular destination for Ivy League graduates, young Chinese flock to apply for jobs at provincial tax bureaus: wide-ranging administrative discretion there almost guarantees lucrative takings.[17] Naked greed trumps public service.

We admit it is a stretch to compare Chinese bureaucrats to Wall Street financiers. Many party officials we met are public-minded people who genuinely care about their country. But the analogy is not exactly off the mark either, at least in the way things are evolving. What should the party leadership do? Some forms of system-tweaking may ease the pressure — most importantly, the astonishingly low salaries of public officials have to be brought up to a level commensurate with their responsibilities — but they will not by themselves get rid of the underlying problem, which is the culture of monetizing power. Institutional remedies can help, but what is really needed is a radical shift in values, based on a clear vision of what constitutes a good government. That is where Confucianism enters.

Two Views of Human Nature

Any discussion of political philosophy must start with an observation of human nature. As James Madison, the "Father of the Constitution," once observed, "[W]hat is government itself, but the greatest of all reflections on human nature?"[18] We want our readers to recall the two contrasting models of human nature we introduced earlier: one based on rational self-interest and the other based on *ren*. For the sake of simplicity, one might say the former is a generally negative view of human nature, while the latter is a more affirmative view. How might these differing views shape political philosophy?

If we assume that human beings are primarily driven by self-interest, we would need to build a political system which controls human behavior by material rewards (carrots) and physical punishment (sticks). Think of US law enforcement, which incarcerates more of its citizens than any other advanced nation.[19] If, on the other hand, we believe that human nature is intrinsically benevolent, then politics would be about encouraging desirable behavior by cultivating the moral character of the people. An example of this line of thinking is Aristotle's purpose of a political community, which he defined as "encouraging goodness" of its citizens.[20] Confucianism, as we shall see shortly, fits into this view.

Which view of human nature is correct? Advances in modern psychology have increasingly shed light on the complex nature of human motivation. Yochai Benkler, an acclaimed researcher of organizational behavior, has identified not one but *four* main drivers of human behavior: material interests, emotional needs, social motivations, and moral commitments.[21] While all four play important roles in our behavior, very often material interests are superseded by the other three. Let us illustrate Benkler's point with one particularly poignant example.

Until the 1970s, most blood donors in America were compensated with cash, while blood donations in Britain were entirely voluntary. The puzzling thing, at least for economists, was that the British system consistently enjoyed higher-quality blood and fewer shortages at hospitals. Then, despite objections by some economists, America transitioned to a volunteer system in the 1970s. Once the material incentives were out of the picture, donations actually *increased* in both quantity and quality. Can rational self-interest explain this result? Of course not. What happened, according to Benkler's analysis, was that the "normative framing" had shifted.[22] If blood donation is framed as a business transaction, one may feel it is okay to be selfish as long as he forgoes the payment. If, on the other hand, the material rewards are out of the picture, one perceives blood donation primarily as a civic duty, and the level of cooperation goes up accordingly. In a study designed to test this hypothesis, researchers asked Swiss villagers whether a nuclear waste dump could be built in their town.[23] When the researchers presented the project as doing a service for the country, more than half of the residents responded in the affirmative. Yet when the residents were told that the parliament had voted to award monetary compensation, only a quarter of them agreed!

It is time we abandoned rational self-interest as the prevailing model of human nature. Under reasonable circumstances, most people would rather be good than selfish. As Ha-Joon Chang puts it, "[I]f you look around and think about it, the world seems to be full of moral behaviours that go against the assumptions of free-market economists".[24] The corollary is that we should trust the humane instincts and the common sense of those around us. In fact, if you assume the best about people, you will often get the best out of them, to your pleasant surprise. The opposite is also true. If you assume the worst about people, you are almost sure to get the worst out of them. Unsurprisingly — although it goes against the standard economic theory — the remarkable incarceration rate in the US has failed to deter crime. The country has higher crime rates than any other comparable country which uses more moderate and tolerant forms of public sanction.[25]

Carrots and sticks may drive human behavior to some degree, but the role of government should be to elevate us *above* them, to make us responsible citizens who can be relied upon to carry out civic duties autonomously. As Michael Sandel, a renowned Harvard professor, observes on the political philosophy of Aristotle,

> The purpose of politics is nothing less than to enable people to develop their distinctive human capabilities and virtues — to deliberate about the common good, to acquire practical judgment, to share in self-government, to care for the community as a whole.[26]

Confucius himself could not have said it better. Let us now lay out the key characteristics of a good government as envisioned by Confucius, which should serve as pragmatic suggestions for fostering a moral culture among politicians and citizens, regardless of the institutional setting.

Characteristics of Good Government

While Confucius never wrote down a systematic summary of his political philosophy, we can discern three common themes which recur throughout the *Analects*: (1) moral rectitude of the leadership; (2) spirit of courtesy (giving way); and (3) maintenance of public trust. All of them are such homely insights that it is a wonder we have to be reminded at all, but the sad truth is that we need them more than ever. Let us illustrate each in turn.

1. Moral rectitude of the leadership

How exactly do we go about effecting a change in culture? Confucius had a simple answer: start from the top. See the following conversation with Lord Chi, then the most powerful man in the state of Lu:

> Lord Chi asked Confucius about governing. Confucius replied, "To govern is to do the right thing. If you as the leader do the right thing, who would dare not do the right thing?" Lord Chi then asked, "I am worried about

the number of thieves in the state. How do I bring them under control?" Confucius replied, "If you as the leader were not greedy, people would not steal, even if you rewarded them for doing so".[27]

Can you feel the power of this short exchange? Basically Confucius is telling Lord Chi, straight to his face: "There are many thieves in our country because you, Sir, are greedy." Confucius was a widely respected teacher at the time, but still we cannot help admiring his courage in confronting his ruler this way. Imagine a modern-day professor of Beijing University admonishing the seven members of the Standing Committee of the Politburo: "If you gentlemen really cleaned up your own acts, including those of your sons and lackeys, which senior official would dare not follow? If senior officials cleaned up their acts, which junior official would dare not follow?"

Until now, the party has tried to deal with the issue of graft through education (Ma De had to watch a documentary film called *Cautionary Lessons* distributed by the anti-graft bureau) and prosecution (the province-level leader featured in the film was executed for embezzling $5 million).[28] Such efforts have all fallen flat. When officials know that graft begins at the very top, how can they take education or prosecution seriously? Solving the issue of corruption is not difficult. If the party leaders actually practiced what they preach, the rank-and-file would naturally fall in line.

Likewise, addressing the role of money in American politics may not be that difficult. Imagine what would have happened if President Obama, during his re-election campaign, had openly renounced all forms of corporate donations and used the bully pulpit of presidency to press his case with the American people. Would Americans have still voted for him? Why not? If the incumbent president shows that a political campaign can succeed without expensive TV ads or deference to wealthy donors, most members of Congress and senators, who are privately fed up with fundraising, will surely follow his lead. Unfortunately, the reality is quite different. President Obama took slack from his own supporters for his "reluctant blessing" of Super PACs, a scheme which allows unlimited donations for a political cause.[29] Under the circumstances, his reluctance to confront this issue head-on may have been understandable, but frankly we hoped for more from the man who had authored *Dreams from My Father* and *Audacity of Hope*. What is needed in American politics right now is not some institutional tinkering but true courage and leadership.

The exchange between Lord Chi and Confucius ends with these memorable words:

> Lord Chi asked Confucius, "What if I executed the bad men, to make lives better for the good ones?" Confucius replied, "Your job is to govern, not to kill. If you desire the good, people would also desire the good. Virtue of the leader is like the wind, and virtue of the people is like grass. Grass bends as the wind blows".[30]

Here Confucius is saying that it is better to lead by example, rather than to force people to change their behavior through persecution. Grass bends as the wind blows. Creating a virtuous society begins at the top.

2. Spirit of courtesy (giving way)

Courtesy is about kindness and consideration. It is about being unselfish and giving way to others. Confucius thought it was the most essential attribute of politics:

> Confucius said, "If the ruler governs with a spirit of courtesy and willingness to give way, what difficulty would there be? If the ruler does not have a spirit of courtesy or willingness to give way, of what use would all the rules of propriety be?"[31]

The willingness to give way is considered the prime virtue of a Confucian gentleman, because governing would be impossible otherwise. Clashes of interests are unavoidable in politics. If political leaders stubbornly protected their positions without yielding an inch, the government would grind to a halt. Someone has to take a step back and offer concessions. If the others follow his example and meet his position halfway, a spirit of cooperation will prevail, and the government will function smoothly.

In America, this ideal of non-adversarial politics is captured in the wistful expression "bipartisanship." We tend to forget, but

American politics has not always been so adversarial. Friedman and Mandelbaum give us the following list of major legislative achievements: the Social Security of Act of 1935; the Federal Aid Highway Act of 1956, which created the inter-state highway system; the Civil Rights Act of 1964; and the Social Security Amendments of 1965, which established Medicare. What do they have in common? All of them passed with a solid majority of *each* party in both the House and the Senate.[32] Such bipartisan cooperation used to be the norm rather than the exception. In fact, it was a necessity. Unlike many democracies of Europe, the American government was built on the principle of the division of power. Unless political leaders were willing to cooperate across party lines, the government could not function.

So why are partisan disputes so bitter now? Some political scientists have suggested that the first-past-the-post (FPTP) voting system, combined with ubiquitous gerrymandering, has contributed to the polarization of the two major parties. Thus, they argue, eliminating FPTP and gerrymandering would alleviate the partisan gridlock. But will such institutional remedies restore responsible policymaking in Washington? They may help, but (as usual) we believe what is really needed is a change in culture. We need to bring back the spirit of courtesy and the virtue of giving way. If this sounds incredibly naïve — if you doubt that "an agenda so simple and straightforward as kindling kindness"[33] could solve the problems of American politics — consider this illuminating example given by Yochai Benkler:

> I was sitting with my kids in the playground. A group of children were digging and playing with trucks in the sandbox. One of the kids was pulling a truck out of another's hands. The two children tugged the truck back and forth until the first child's mother intervened, explaining patiently that he should share his toy nicely with the others. He let go of the truck and was rewarded with a toothy grin from the other child and a warm, approving look from his mother.[34]

The irony of this heart-warming scene, notes Benkler, is that this was downtown Manhattan, the dog-eat-dog centre of commerce. The boy's mother who intervened had the look of an investment banker or a lawyer. Had she conducted her business negotiations in the same way that she taught her child, she would not have survived the merciless competition of her profession. And yet there she was, teaching her child to be kind and considerate, as most mothers in her situation would. The lesson of this little tale is that it is actually quite *natural* for us to act generously. How many times have we seen strangers voluntarily giving way, holding doors, or helping with heavy luggage? If we take such unselfish behavior for granted in our private lives, why not demand the same of our public sphere?

Modern politics (not just in America) is characterized by endless wrangling between political parties. So-called leaders maliciously attack and even hurl slanders at one another. The resulting hostility between the competing parties forestalls any mutually acceptable solution. Amidst all the sound and fury, the only winners are the super-empowered special interests, who merrily play one party against the other. The vast majority of the electorate, who usually hold moderate and centrist views, are left in quiet despair.[35] We are saying that things do not have to be this way. We can and should elevate politics above childlike ego-centricism ("That truck is *mine!*"). Human nature is better than that. Isn't it about time we rediscovered the virtue of giving way ("Be nice and share the truck.") and restored civility to our political discourse?

3. Maintenance of public trust

Public trust is defined as the trust people place in their government. Confucius taught that upholding it is the utmost priority of government:

> Zigong asked about government. Confucius said, "Government should provide abundant food, a sufficient army, and trust for the people." Zigong asked again, "If it cannot be helped, which one of the three may be dispensed with?" Confucius replied, "Throw away the army." Zigong asked yet again, "If it cannot be helped, which one of the last two may be sacrificed?" Confucius replied, "Give up on the food. From of old, people have died one way or the other. But if trust breaks down, the society cannot stand."[36]

Here Confucius indicates that, broadly speaking, a government has three priorities: economy (food), defence (army), and public trust. All three are important. Still, if we had to choose one, public trust comes first. Confucius is not denying the importance of the other two. Rather, he is calling attention to the fact that intangible confidence is a more essential foundation of society than physical conditions such as the economy and the military.

Nothing erodes public trust faster than lies by politicians. The worst recent example must be that of Russia, where President Medvedev announced that Putin would replace him after the presidential election in March 2012. Incredibly, Medvedev explained that the "job swap" had been pre-agreed several years ago, essentially admitting that his presidency was nothing more than a charade — making a mockery of the 50 million people who had voted for him four years earlier. *The Economist* described the farce as follows: "the arrival of the genuine official [i.e. Putin] was announced by the pretender, and the pair hugged in front of duped bureaucrats who rewarded them with a standing ovation for their clever performance".[37] The consequence was predictable: hundreds of thousands of mostly middle-class Muscovites took to the streets in the largest mass protests Russia has seen in two decades. Putin may have given them a prosperous economy and a strong army, but repeated lying by the leaders has broken the bond of trust beyond repair.

Russia may seem like a distant example to our Western readers, but then the state of democracy today is hardly comforting. Brazen lies by politicians masquerade as election strategy, a phenomenon which the Nobel laureate Paul Krugman dubbed "post-truth politics".[38] Mitt Romney, the Republican presidential candidate during the last election, is a sad example. In the primary race, he pushed cynical pragmatism to a new height by obsessively hiding his beliefs and saying just about anything he thought would get him the nomination. In an attempt to appease the conservative wing of his party, he switched his past positions on such major issues as abortion, climate change, healthcare, and taxes. Once he secured the nomination, he went on to attack President Obama with plain falsehoods and misleading statements. It was distressing to see him stoop so low, as the man is obviously gifted, with extraordinary achievements in both the public and private sectors.

But then Romney was only building on a tradition started by George W. Bush. Remember the "Swift Boat Veterans for Truth," which smeared the 2004 presidential candidate, John Kerry? Or the vicious personal attacks on John McCain (the "Manchurian Candidate"), his wife Cindy (the "drug addict"), and even their adopted daughter ("born out of wedlock") during the crucial South Carolina primary in 2000?[39] Was it any surprise that Bush, once he entered the Oval Office, would bend the intelligence about weapons of mass destruction (WMDs)? How much credibility has the lie cost the US government, when it was finally revealed that WMDs did not exist in Iraq?

The key point here is that public trust is a precious thing which we must cherish and protect above all else. In order to do so, politicians must not lie, and the government must not cover things up. For too long, we have taken it for granted that the expediency of statecraft takes precedence over truth (think of all the "classified" information). Confucius is telling us the opposite: *nothing* takes precedence over truth in politics.

Freedom of the Media

Public trust is the bedrock of a nation. Without it, even the best democracy falls apart; with it, a dictatorship can flourish. What lesson should Beijing draw here? We mentioned that ordinary Chinese, even though they often hold local bureaucrats in contempt, largely trust their leaders in Beijing. There are two explanations for this benign view: first, the government has consistently delivered on its social development goals; second, the leaders, even as their private lives are often marred by infighting and graft, do seem to have the best interest of the country in their minds. The first is about competence, and the second is about good intentions. Both are important pillars of public trust. All the same, we suggest that the Chinese leadership seriously consider introducing a third pillar: freedom of the media.

During the aforementioned baby milk scandal, it was the local government which pressured the Sanlu management to conceal it for almost one year, because they feared the news might smear the PR efforts in the run-up to the Olympics. The resulting delay ended up affecting the health of an estimated 300,000 babies. Is this any way to engender trust? More recently, a collision between two trains on the newly built high-speed railway caused considerable embarrassment. Not only did it reveal rampant corruption inside the Railways Ministry, but the hesitant and half-hearted coverage by the state media drew heavy criticism. As one disillusioned blogger puts it, "I just watched the news on the train crash in Wenzhou, but I feel like I still don't even know what happened. Nothing is reliable anymore... Is there anything that we can still trust?"[40]

Official media sources do not inspire trust in China, because it is customary for the central propaganda department to censor articles and issue reporting guidelines. According to online leaks, the department issued the following directive shortly after the accident:

> Latest demands on the Wenzhou train collision accident: 1. Figures on the number of dead must follow numbers from authoritative departments; 2. Frequency of reports must not be too dense; 3. More reporting should be done on stories that are extremely moving, for example people donating blood and taxi drivers not accepting fares; 4. There must be no seeking after the causes [of the accident], rather, statements from authoritative departments must be followed; 5. No looking back and no commentary.[41]

In the face of a deadly crash which officially claimed 40 lives and injured 191 others, the propaganda department was basically saying: Let's not make a big deal out of it. Do not investigate who is to blame. Do not challenge official reports. Do not write opinion pieces on it. Divert people's attention with soapy human drama. How would the victims and their families feel about such a whitewash? Is it any wonder that official reporting of the event was met with widespread anger and suspicion? Nothing can be hidden in this age of the Internet. All the cover-up does is to undermine the party's standing with its people. Is it not time that the party leadership changed tactics and recognized that honesty is indeed the best policy?

Let us mention three reasons to believe that a free media is necessary for China. First, it will force the state media to be more forthcoming, while also instilling the habit of telling truths in the ranks of civil servants. Over the long term, this will strengthen rather than weaken the bond of trust between the party and the people.

Second, as China grapples with the issues of local corruption and environmental pollution, the role of a free media will be indispensable. Without the help of investigative journalists, Beijing cannot effectively monitor and respond to what is happening on the ground, because local bureaucrats cannot be counted on to report the problems they themselves have caused.

The third, more subtle reason is that a free media will unleash creativity within the population. In recent years, the so-called "Korean wave" of pop music and television dramas has swept across Asia, partly because South Korea enjoys more freedom of media than any other Asian country. As The Economist observes, "Eventually people [of Asia] may start to get the real message of the links between the country's prosperity, openness, relative political freedom and lively — if nakedly commercial — popular culture."[42] We have also seen the opposite case in Hong Kong, which used to be the creative hub of the Chinese-speaking world. Its filmmaking industry prospered because Hong Kong enjoyed unrestricted freedom of expression as a British colony. Then, sometime around the handover to China, the industry suffered a drastic decline, and many of its star actors and filmmakers emigrated abroad. The undeniable lesson here is that thoughts cannot flourish under censorship. The party must learn to let go of its controls. That is the only way it can, to borrow an old socialist slogan, "let a hundred flowers bloom" in the arts and academics.

We do not hold a naïve view of free media. Too often, freedom of the media degenerates into freedom of rich media owners to manipulate public opinion. For instance, News Corporation, the media conglomerate which owns Fox News and the Wall Street Journal, has repeatedly questioned the science of climate change, thereby sowing doubt among the public. The anti-scientific propaganda benefited Big Oil by forestalling environmental regulations. The problem here is that Rupert Murdoch, the founder and chairman of News Corporation, is a personal investor in the oil sector (alongside former vice president Dick Cheney).[43] So what is good for Exxon Mobil and Koch Industries may also be good for Rupert Murdoch. This is a clear conflict of interest, but as we have seen in the recent phone hacking scandal, the Murdochs are not exactly the kind of people who worry about morality (or even legality) in their media activities.

Still, even if we accept that freedom of the media is not unquestionably good, the best way for China to combat the tyranny of media barons is not to censor media, but to have a true public voice of its own. A good example to follow would be that of Britain. Despite fierce competition from its private-sector rivals, the BBC remains extremely popular in Britain, with its news enjoying a market share of 47%.[44] While the BBC may not be as sensational as the tabloids, the British simply trust it more as "the narrator of the national story".[45] Can China Central Television (CCTV) become just as popular, trustworthy, and respectable? We certainly think so. For that to happen, though, the party must allow the journalists to do their jobs.

Learn from Singapore

Among the "post-Confucian" societies of Asia, Singapore is probably the most natural model for China to emulate, not only because the two countries share similar cultures (74% of Singaporeans are ethnic Chinese), but also because the People's Action Party of Singapore has been in power for almost as long as the Chinese Communist Party. During the legendary 1992 tour of southern China, Deng Xiaoping famously remarked: "There is good social order in Singapore... We should draw from their experience, and do even better than them".[46] Party officials have taken this advice to heart, regularly visiting Singapore to observe and learn the best practices. In the booming cities of southern China, governance manuals such as *Why Can Singapore Do It?* have become bestsellers.[47] Lee Kuan Yew, the founding father of modern Singapore, is probably the only world leader who commands as much respect in Beijing and Moscow as he does in London and Washington.

Just how successful has Singapore been? The city-state is currently ranked the world's fourth leading financial center, after London, New York, and Hong Kong (*Global Financial Centres Index* by the City of London); the most competitive economy in the world (*Doing Business Report* by the World Bank); and the country with the highest proportion of millionaires in the world, surpassing Switzerland and Qatar (*Global Wealth Report* by the Boston Consulting Group). It is these singular economic achievements which make Singapore anathema to defenders of Western-style democracy — and the darling of the single-party dictatorship in Beijing.

But then Singapore is hardly the only authoritarian state which has thrived. Michael Schuman gives the following table of "miracle" economies in his book *The Miracle: The Epic Story of Asia's Quest for Wealth.*[48]

Growth of National Income per Capita (in current US dollars)

Country	1965	2007	Percent change
South Korea	130	19,690	15,046%
Taiwan	204	15,078	7,291%
Singapore	540	32,470	5,913%
Hong Kong	710	31,610	4,352%
Japan	890	37,670	4,133%
Thailand	130	3,400	2,515%
China	100	2,360	2,260%
Indonesia*	70	1,650	2,257%
Malaysia	330	6,540	1,882%
India	110	950	764%

*Earliest year available is 1969.
Source: World Bank; Taiwan Directorate General of Budget, Accounting and Statistics.

Can you guess how many of the 10 countries above were considered a liberal democracy during the period of hyper-charged growth? The answer might surprise you: one. Four countries in the table had outright dictatorships (South Korea, Taiwan, China, and Indonesia).

Three had democratic institutions, but in reality were one-party states (Japan, Singapore, and Malaysia). Thailand had periods of military rule, and Hong Kong was a colony.[49] Only India had a true multi-party democracy, and its economic performance, impressive as it is, has been laggard compared with those of the Asian Tigers.

Given the above, it was inevitable that some people would start to see a link between rapid industrialization and authoritarianism, in what came to be known as the "developmental dictatorship" thesis. The theory quickly fell out of favor, though, because authoritarian states elsewhere in the world were obviously not growing as fast (think of the Middle East and Sub-Saharan Africa). It was further undermined by the fact that at least five "miracle" countries have since become full-fledged democracies, with multiple parties competing for power (South Korea, Taiwan, Japan, Thailand, and Indonesia).

The more plausible explanations are the "Asian model" and "Asian values" theories. The former is an institutional argument, while the latter is a cultural one. The "Asian model" theory says that an activist state is more conducive to early industrialization than a purely *laissez-faire* state, because infant industries can be "nurtured" through subsidies and trade barriers. The theory has been highly influential, but it faces the problem that China and India have achieved high growth primarily by relaxing, not tightening, the government's grips on the economy.[50] The main advocate of the "Asian values" theory has been none other than Lee Kuan Yew, who attributed the remarkable success of the Asian Tigers to their Confucian culture — a culture which is characterized by devotion to education, a spirit of self-sacrifice, and social cohesion based on common norms. As he told Fareed Zakaria, the Indian-American journalist, in a 1994 interview,

> [Other developing countries] will not succeed in the same way as East Asia did because certain driving forces will be absent. If you have a culture that doesn't place much value in learning and scholarship and hard work and thrift... the going will be much slower.[51]

The problem with Lee's theory, however, is that not all "miracle" economies are Confucian. While the first wave of the Asian miracle was indeed driven by Confucian societies — Japan, South Korea, Taiwan, Hong Kong, and Singapore — the miracle has since spread across the continent, to Thailand (Buddhism), India (Hinduism), Malaysia and Indonesia (Islam).[52]

We believe both the Asian model and Asian values theories contain elements of truth. Even the "developmental dictatorship" thesis is valid to the extent that a dictatorship can be more effective at forcing necessary sacrifices and enacting long-term policies. But we would like to offer a simpler explanation for the Asian miracle: the quality of leadership, which is another way of saying that it is all about people. Schuman comes to the same conclusion, and devotes his book to recounting the stories of great leaders who made the miracle happen: Hayato Ikeda, the principal architect of Japan's industrial policy; Park Chung-hee, the iron-fisted general who industrialized Korea; Deng Xiaoping, who lifted a billion people out of poverty; and, of course, Lee Kuan Yew, for whom it is hard to invent a new accolade. (Henry Kissinger once said, "I've not learned as much from anybody as I have from Mr. Lee Kuan Yew".[53] Margaret Thatcher put it more simply: "He was never wrong".[54])

All of which leads us back to the earlier question: How does Singapore do it? It is not just economic wealth which impresses visitors to Singapore. The Singaporean government excels in almost every area one can think of: The country enjoys a low tax rate and a balanced budget. Its streets are clean, and its roads are nearly congestion-free. The city is a model for urban planning and public housing, with no slum to be found anywhere. No country manages water resources better, or treats waste more efficiently. Its education system is the best in the world according to the Trends in International Mathematics and Science Study (TIMSS), and just as impressive is the quality of its vocational training for less gifted students. The country boasts excellent healthcare, as evidenced by the lowest infant mortality in the world. It also has a well-designed public pension system, which induces citizens to build and manage personal assets. Can we explain all of this in terms of authoritarianism versus democracy, state interference versus laissez-faire, city-state versus large state, or any other institutional factor? We think not.

The true lesson of Singapore, for China and the rest of the world, is this: no other government takes people development more seriously. The closest parallel we can think of is not with any other government but with the best private-sector employers such as McKinsey and Goldman Sachs. As *The Economist* observes,

> Sitting around a table with its 30-something mandarins is more like meeting junior partners at Goldman Sachs or McKinsey than the cast of "Yes, Minister." The person on your left is on secondment at a big oil company; on your right sits a woman who between spells at the finance and defence ministries has picked up degrees from the London School of Economics, Cambridge and Stanford. High-fliers pop in and out of the Civil Service College for more training; the prime minister has written case studies for them. But it is not a closed shop. Talent from the private sector is recruited into both the civil service and politics.[55]

Civil service candidates are spotted early on and are carefully groomed before being picked up by various ministries. Those who do not make the cut are weeded out. The recruiting process of the People's Action Party is similarly rigorous. Candidates, many of whom have already demonstrated excellence in the private sector, are put through a gruelling series of interviews and even psychological tests which are meant to expose their most deeply held values.[56] The relentless focus on people results in a high level of competence throughout the government.

It also ensures that the government is free of corruption. As Lee categorically declares, "You need people who are inoculated against corruption... Once we are corrupt, we are finished".[57] Singapore has succeeded because its leaders are not only able but also honest and selfless. Lee is a stoic individual who has lived in the same family house since the 1940s, without bothering to renovate it. Likewise, many other leaders have chosen politics over lucrative private careers (the current defense minister was a top surgeon, for example) because of their sense of honor and *noblesse oblige*. We are aware of the shortcomings of Singapore — most importantly, high income inequality and limited freedom of expression — but the caliber of its leaders inspires us nonetheless.

* * *

The whole purpose of Confucian teachings was to create exemplary leaders, so that their civic virtue would permeate ("trickle down to") the entire society. Confucians did not worry too much about institution-building *per se* because, in the end, it was the *people* who managed the system. To the Confucians, the inner morality of the people who managed the system mattered more than the system itself. As Hsun Tzu memorably put it, "There is no such thing as a disorderly system of state; only disorderly rulers exist. There is no such thing as an orderly system of law; only orderly citizens exist".[58] As such, their approach was the polar opposite of those taken by such Enlightenment thinkers as John Locke, who advocated a division of power to render the system as "fool-proof" as possible. Both approaches have their respective strengths and weaknesses, and surely some combination of both will be needed to achieve optimal outcomes in modern society. All the same, we believe it is time that we shifted our focus from democratic institution-building to the moral quality of leadership.

Democracy is not an end in and of itself. It is merely a means of putting the right leaders in charge and, as Singapore demonstrates, there are other ways to achieve the same goal. How many times have we seen a democratic movement turn to tears when the elected leaders turned out to be incompetent, corrupt, or both? Remember the Orange Revolution? While we surely appreciate the effectiveness of elective democracy in preventing the worst excesses of power, we must also recognize the value of the meritocratic, education-driven approach which Confucianism advocates. After all, we truly need our governments to be smart and efficient, if we are to have any hope of tackling the daunting economic and environmental challenges of our time. If a little city-state with 3.2 million citizens can pull its best and brightest to create a world-class administration, why can't much larger states do the same?

More than anything else, Confucianism is a philosophy for developing moral leadership, as we shall see later in the chapter on education. But an unfortunate consequence of the emphasis on people and the associated lack of attention on institutional safeguards was that Confucianism never gave birth to the notion of constitutional rights, or other forms of checks on absolutist power, as transpired in the West. We are not denying the importance of institution-building here. But as the limits of purely institution-driven political reforms are becoming clear, Confucianism may well become relevant again as a philosophy for instilling the right political culture and cultivating the right kind of leaders.

Chapter

3

On the Economy

Mencius went to see King Hui of Liang, who said, "Sir, since you have not counted it far to come here, a distance of a thousand leagues, may I presume that you can offer counsels to profit my kingdom?" Mencius replied, "Why must your Majesty speak of profit? What I can provide are counsels to benevolence and righteousness, and they are my only topics."

Mencius, 1a-1

Laissez-faire versus Social Realization

The expression *"laissez-faire"* comes from a French phrase meaning "Let [it] be." Legend has it that Jean-Baptiste Colbert, the French finance minister best known for pioneering mercantilism, met a group of business owners in 1680. When Colbert asked how the government could help their businesses, the leader of the group quipped, "Let us be." We do not know whether that moment marked the birth of *laissez-faire*, but the episode captures the essence of its non-interventionist philosophy. In modern times, the term mainly refers to freedom from state interference in the economic realm. It also denotes the doctrine of having a smaller government in general, as captured in Henry David Thoreau's famous dictum: "That government is best which governs least."

So it is perhaps surprising to learn that the *laissez-faire* philosophy of governing (although not the term itself) existed 2,500 years ago. The philosopher who expounded the idea was Lao Tzu, the ancient sage of Taoism. The entire philosophy of Lao Tzu can be summed up in one sentence: Let it be. To see how this principle is applied to government, take a look at the following verse from *Tao Te Ching*, which many view as the most beautiful and profound work ever written in the Chinese language[1]:

> The best government is when people only know that rulers exist. The next best is when people love and praise their rulers. The next is when people fear their rulers. The next is when people feel humiliated by their rulers.[2]

Some scholars (incorrectly) translate the opening phrase as "people do not even know that rulers exist",[3] but anyway the meaning is the same. The best government is all but invisible to its citizens. People know it exists, but state interference is so minimal that they lead their daily lives without ever worrying about it. The next best is a paternalistic government, which people love and praise for its compassionate efforts. Lao Tzu was already an old man when Confucius was born, so he could not have had Confucianism in mind when he wrote the verse above, but it is exactly the kind of benevolent government with which Confucianism is closely associated. Next in line is a legalistic government, in which an intimidating authority (the Hobbesian Leviathan) imposes order by threatening people with legal enforcement. Lastly, according to Lao Tzu, the worst form of government is an arbitrary dictatorship, where so-called leaders insult the dignity of their citizens by taking their lives and property at will. Under the legalistic government, at least a semblance of order is maintained; under the arbitrary dictatorship, life is genuinely nasty, brutish, and short.

Why did Lao Tzu prefer *laissez-faire* to paternalism? For much the same reason that neoclassical economists advocate free-market capitalism today: good intention *distorts*. Whenever a government tries to do something good, it necessarily ends up favoring one particular person or a section of the society over all the others. But a government must not play favorites. Better to have a government which acts as a fair referee to everyone.

This line of thought is consistent with the rest of Lao Tzu's philosophy. In another verse, Lao Tzu categorically states that "nature is not benevolent".[4] Unlike Rousseau who romanticized nature, Lao Tzu saw nature as impersonal and merciless. Who could disagree, seeing all the floods, hurricanes, earthquakes, and volcanic eruptions? Yet because nature has no mercy toward any particular individual, it is also reliable and fair. As Wang Bi (AD 226–249), a boy prodigy who left the most authoritative commentaries on *Tao Te Ching* and *I Ching*, observes,

> Nature just lets itself be. It doesn't act or manipulate... That is why [Lao Tzu says] nature is not benevolent. Benevolence necessarily manipulates, takes sides, gives favours, and makes alterations... Such acts distort the true nature of things.

Wang Bi was in his teens when he wrote these profound words. His Mozart-like genius is a fascinating topic by itself — anyone who has actually tried to make sense of *I Ching* will understand what we mean — but what concerns us here is why Confucians defied the sagely wisdom and embraced a more activist approach. We find a clue in Han Yu's *Study of the Way*, the Tang-era treatise which triggered a backlash against Taoism and Buddhism — and eventually served as the precursor to Neo-Confucianism.

> [The "sage kings" of ancient China] are sometimes called emperors, at other times kings. Appellations may differ, but their sagehood is the same [i.e. they all endeavoured to better the lives of the people.] During the summer we can wear linen, but during the winter we must wear fur. When we are thirsty, a glass of water will do, but when we are hungry, we must eat well. Circumstances may differ, but their wisdom is the same. Nowadays intellectuals, who wallow in Taoism and Buddhism, will say, "Why not learn the ancient wisdom of leaving things alone?" This is like saying to those who desperately seek fur in wintertime, "Why not put on linen?", or telling those who suffer from hunger, "Why not drink a glass of water?"[5]

What drove Han Yu was his concern for people's livelihood. Like other pre-modern societies, China had to endure occasional bouts of widespread famine, which could be caused by any number of reasons: wars, droughts, epidemics, locusts, or the plain idiocy of the bureaucrats. Confronted with an impending calamity, how could one just sit still and let things be? Winter in northern China was brutal, especially for those who could not afford firewood and warm clothing. Ian Morris, in his account of the period, quotes a poem which describes a woman so desperate for firewood that she sells her body: "Didn't you see her, last winter, when travellers were stopped by rain and snow… At twilight she knocked on the gate, but no one wanted her trade".[6] In the face of such obvious human tragedy, *laissez-faire* would be nothing other than irresponsibility. That is why Han Yu advocated a more paternalistic approach to governance, based on compassion and righteousness, calling for a society where "the widows, the elderly, the orphans, the disabled, and the sick are taken care of".[7]

In his last passage, Han Yu is making a reference to Mencius's conversation with King Hsuan of Chi, where Mencius suggests that widows, orphans, and the elderly without children are "the most destitute of people who have no one to lean on," and a benevolent ruler must take care of them.[8] Mencius further asserts that "an intelligent ruler would manage the livelihood of people" so that "grey-haired men will not be seen on the streets carrying heavy burdens on their backs".[9] Concern for social welfare was the hallmark of a Confucian gentleman. In fact, the very notion of Confucian sagehood rested upon it, as the following exchange in the *Analects* shows:

> Zigong asked, "Suppose someone improved the wellbeing of people, and rescued those in need, what would you say of him? Would you say such a person possesses *ren*?" Confucius replied, "Why only speak of *ren*? That person must be a saint. Even Yao and Shun [the "sage kings" of ancient China] have struggled with this".[10]

This is an unexpected reply, because we normally associate sainthood with holy men who embody religious virtues. Here, Confucius is saying that the true saint is not some ascetic who meditates for years on a mountaintop, but a worldly leader who benefits the society at large. The former only seeks salvation for himself, while the latter seeks salvation for all, which we will henceforth refer to as

"social realization." For Confucius, social realization was the ultimate expression of *ren*: "A man of *ren*, wishing to stand himself, also
helps others stand. Wishing to succeed himself, he also helps others
succeed".[11] The man of *ren* could not be selfish. What would be the
point of compassion, aesthetic sensibility, and humaneness, if such
qualities did not lead one to care about the hungry and the homeless
around him? Therein lay the case for a paternalistic government. It
was all about possessing a warm heart. Even Wang Bi once admitted
that although he subscribed to Taoist philosophy, he admired
Confucius more than Lao Tzu as a human being.

Before we embark on our exploration of modern capitalism, let
us consider these unforgettable opening words of Victor Hugo's *Les
Misérables*, which capture the necessity of social realization today just
as well as they did 150 years ago:

> So long as there shall exist, by reason of law and custom, a social con-
> demnation, which, in the face of civilization, artificially creates a hell on
> earth... so long as the three problems of this age — the degradation of man
> by poverty, the ruin of woman by starvation, and the dwarfing of childhood
> by physical and spiritual night — are not yet solved... so long as ignorance
> and misery remain on earth, books like this cannot be useless.[12]

While capitalism is a generally wonderful concept, which is
demonstrably effective at creating wealth and unlocking human
potential, it must be balanced by the humanity (*ren*) of its participants. Without such balancing, a purely market-based system quickly
degenerates into cutthroat, no-holds-barred competition which
allows the strong to ruthlessly take advantage of the weak and
thereby "artificially creates a hell on earth" for most people. In this
chapter, we will illustrate the dehumanizing aspects of free-market
capitalism and lay out a more humane alternative.

Misery of the Middle Class

In recent years, we have seen a flurry of articles and books about the
failures of capitalism, especially the Anglo-Saxon variety which
advocates tax cuts, deregulation, privatization, and free trade — in

short, policies which uphold the sanctity of free markets. Even before the global financial crisis, Elizabeth Warren and Amelia Tyagi called attention to the dire state of the American middle class in *The Two-Income Trap: Why Middle-Class Parents Are Going Broke*, and Jared Bernstein criticized the YOYO ("You're on your own") ideology of market fundamentalists in his much-cited book *All Together Now: Common Sense for a Fair Economy*. More recently, public health experts Richard Wilkinson and Kate Picket documented the pernicious social effects of income inequality in *The Spirit Level: Why Greater Equality Makes Societies Stronger*, and Ha-Joon Chang ripped apart common assumptions of neoclassical economics in *23 Things They Don't Tell You about Capitalism*. Books exposing the hypocrisy of Wall Street are too numerous to mention, although John Bogle's *Enough* stands out because of who the author is (the founder of Vanguard, which manages a mind-numbing $1.7 trillion in assets).

It is not just leftists who are raising questions. Charles Murray, the darling of right-wing conservatives, made class division the subject of his latest bestseller *Coming Apart: The State of White America, 1960–2010*, although the half-hearted remedies he proposes would hardly assuage the concerns of the Occupy Wall Street protesters.[13] More serious academics who voiced concern are listed by Thomas Edsall, an acclaimed journalist, in an online post titled "Is This the End of Market Democracy?"

> [Fundamental questions on free-market capitalism] are matters of concern to many highly respected experts — people not known for leftist jeremiads. Among them are Jeffrey Sachs, a professor at Columbia University; Nobel Prize winner Michael Spence; Francis Fukuyama, senior fellow at Stanford's Center on Democracy; former Treasury Secretary Lawrence Summers; and three of the nation's foremost labor economists, Richard Freeman and Lawrence Katz, both of Harvard, and David Autor of M.I.T.[14]

Why are all these distinguished scholars suddenly anguishing over the viability of capitalism? Did not the triumph over communism in the 20th century prove once and for all that capitalism is the superior form of economic organization? Part of the answer lies in the moral bankruptcy of the financial services industry, which the global financial crisis has amply demonstrated. We will return to the issue of the erosion of ethics shortly. The more pressing concern, however, is the rising income inequality and the associated economic insecurity of the middle class. Just how bad is the situation?

To get a sense of the crisis, let us turn to the heartbreaking account given by Elizabeth Warren in her memorable 2007 lecture, "The Coming Collapse of the Middle Class." (You can view it on YouTube. It will be 45 minutes well spent.) Before being elected to the Senate, Warren was a bankruptcy law expert at Harvard Law School. In the late 1990s, she noticed an astonishing rise of personal bankruptcy. Specifically, the number of women filing for bankruptcy rose from around 69,000 in 1981 to nearly half a million in 1999.[15] It prompted her to study the income and consumption patterns of a "typical" American family, with a median household income and two children. The most obvious trend was a precipitous fall in the savings rate (from around 11% in 1972 to *negative* 0.8% in 2006) combined with a drastic rise in debt (e.g. credit card debt has risen from 1.4% of annual income to about 15% over the same period). Why have Americans grown so indebted?

The popular explanation is that Americans have become profligate. This is a view advanced by the likes of Charles Murray, who contends that the cultural decline of the working class is largely responsible for their economic plight. Warren shows that nothing can be further from the truth. A middle-class family in America spends *less* than it used to on discretionary items such as clothing (down by 34% from a generation ago), food (–18%), and appliances (–52%). So why are scrimping Americans falling deeper into debt? It is because of the rise in essential expenditures, such as housing (+76%), health insurance (+74%), and childcare (up by more than 100%). And it is not as if Americans are buying bigger houses or getting better healthcare than before. An "average" house in the early 1970s had 5.8 rooms, including bathrooms; now it has 6.1 rooms and is probably older (over 50% of the middle class live in houses built more than 25 years ago). The quality of healthcare has deteriorated in the sense that hospitals discharge patients more quickly

("Send them home sicker and quicker," to use a cynical industry expression). Even worse, many families can only afford "false" insurance, which covers "everything" except hospitalization, specialists, and prescription drugs.

The stunning result of the rise in essential expenditures is that a median household in America has less disposable income than it did a generation ago, despite the fact that most families now have two income-earners rather than just one. That is why Americans are forced to economize on non-essential items such as clothing, food, and appliances. The burden falls especially heavily on families with children, since they pay disproportionately more for housing (to be near decent public schools), childcare, and education. When couples with children buy expensive suburban homes, they are really "buying education" because public schools are assigned by zip codes. One might ask, "But why spend so much on education?" Well, they have to. Back in the 1970s, one could easily enter the middle class with a high-school diploma and a good work ethic. Today, most people (rightly) believe that a college degree is "the single ticket to the middle class."

Now, think of what happens when a highly leveraged company also has high fixed costs: it is more likely to go bankrupt. The same principle applies to family finance. Families with children (who have high fixed costs) are more than *twice* as likely to file for bankruptcy as those without. Because one paycheck cannot cover all their fixed costs, they run out of money rapidly if either of the two income-earners suffers a job loss, or if any family member runs into a serious medical problem. Warren gives this poignant example: back in the days when only the father was working, the mother could care for the child if the child fell ill. Nowadays, "Mom stays at the hospital with her child until she loses her job." A medical problem of a family member is one of the three leading causes of bankruptcy in America, alongside job loss and family break-up. Add to this the fact that the volatility of family income — i.e. the risk of losing a job — roughly doubled between 1973 and 2004 (according to a study by Jacob Hacker of Yale University), and it is no wonder that bankruptcy filings and mortgage foreclosures have soared.

Having laid out the depressing state of the American middle class, Warren concludes:

> I fear we are moving from a three-class society to a two-class society. We actually are going to see a larger upper class, we are seeing them, not just the rich-rich, but the sort of rich, the ones who have those same jobs, bring in two incomes, who don't get sick, who don't lose their jobs... who don't divorce, who don't have a death in the family, who don't hit any of life's problems. They stay within the upper group, they put away some savings, they don't get deep in debt, they do okay. And then the rest is just one long trail of underclass that stays on a constant debt treadmill, sometimes it's a little more, sometimes it's a little less, but never out of debt, never [with] any real economic security. I could change my metaphors: people who are just constantly living on the edge of a cliff, some falling over, some scratching back up a little, but never with the kind of security that for the first three quarters of the century we associated with being middle class.[16]

Breakdown of Morality

While the middle class hovers on the edge of misery, the top 1% (or 0.1%, to be more precise) is doing better than ever. At the extreme end, the top 25 hedge fund managers raked in $22 billion in 2010.[17] Since the median personal income in the US is around $40,000, it means that these lucky individuals made as much as 550,000 typical Americans combined. To add insult to injury, they pay lower taxes as a percentage of their income than middle-class workers do. Under a strange loophole in the American tax law, the performance fee of hedge fund managers ("carried interest" in industry jargon) is treated as a capital gain, which is taxable at a maximum rate of 15%.

One might ask, "But aren't those fund managers creating that much value?" That is doubtful. Hedge funds trade stocks, bonds, commodities, and other liquid assets. Any trade has a buyer and a seller. If a hedge fund manager makes money by selling a stock at just the right time, it means that whoever bought the stock got into the market at the wrong time. Any winning trade creates a loser at the other end. It is a zero-sum game, just like Baccarat. The only social value we can think of is that hedge funds bring greater liquidity to the market because they trade so frequently. But that is a very marginal benefit to justify such outsized paychecks. Some argue that hedge funds help allocate capital better, but it is more plausible that the extremely short-term outlook of hedge fund managers hurts rather than benefits the overall economy. To sum up: the only reason these 25 individuals do so well is that they gamble with other people's money very well.

At least these hedge fund managers can claim that they have not lost their investors' money. The more egregious examples involve CEOs who destroyed shareholder value and profited handsomely in the process. John Bogle singles out three financial sector CEOs: Charles Prince of Citigroup, who was paid $138 million during his disastrous four-year tenure which saw the company write off some $21 billion as losses; Stanley O'Neil of Merrill Lynch, who earned $161 million (and gained retirement benefits worth $160 million on top of it) while the company's stock price tumbled from $95 per share to $20; and James Cayne of Bear Stearns, who had been paid $232 million before the company went under and was subsequently rescued by the Federal Reserve and JPMorgan Chase.[18] How can the leaders of failing companies be paid so well? The reason is that they enjoy performance bonuses while the times are good, but they do not cough up those earnings when the times turn sour. All the above-mentioned CEOs adopted risky strategies in order to boost earnings (and their pay) in the short term. When the reckoning finally came, forcing the banks to write off tens of billions in bad assets, they duly resigned. But they were not required to pay back any of the bonuses, a perverse system of incentives which Bogle condemns as "Heads I win, tails you lose."

The breakdown of morality in the financial services industry was well captured by Greg Smith, the author of *Why I Left Goldman Sachs*. He laments that the firm has lost its long-standing culture of doing right by its clients, and focuses instead on milking as much money off of them as it can. In internal communications, the clients are often referred to as "muppets" (marionette puppets), implying they are objects of manipulation. One of the surest ways to win promotion is to execute "axes," Goldman-speak for the practice of force-feeding clients products that nobody wants.[19] It brings to mind a scene from the movie *Margin Call*, where a conflicted executive (Sam) objects to an order from the bank president (John) that he dump all the toxic securities into the market.[20]

Sam: The real question is, who are we selling this to?

John: The same people we've been selling it to for the last two years, and whoever else would buy it.

Sam: But John, if you do this, you will kill the market for years. It's over. And you're selling something that you know has no value.

John: We are selling to willing buyers at the current fair market price.

Here Sam is protesting that, by selling papers he knows are worthless, he will be duping his clients. John's reply is that the buyers are suckers, client interest be damned. While the act of selling to willing buyers may not be illegal, this kind of mentality is clearly unbecoming of a professional, whose key attribute is "commitment to the interest of clients in particular, and the welfare of society in general".[21] Bogle points out that it is not just the financial industry professionals whose values are being undermined. Profession after profession, the bottom-line society of ours is driving an increasing number of accountants, lawyers, journalists, and even doctors to ditch professional codes of conduct.[22] The single-minded pursuit of profit, combined with the associated erosion of morality, is a pervasive phenomenon which is not restricted to the upper echelons of the financial services industry.

In the meantime, those in the middle class toil away, trying to make ends meet in an era of ever-rising costs (childcare for two children can easily cost $15,000 a year in coastal cities in the US) and stagnant wages (the real hourly wage for a typical male in America fell from $15.76 in 1973 to $15.62 in 2005).[23] Something is wrong with this picture. Jared Bernstein points out in *All Together Now* that, during the 1973–2005 period when the typical earnings of a male worker went nowhere, the overall economy grew by 150% and productivity increased by 80%.[24] The situation bears an eerie resemblance to England during the industrial revolution: its output per worker grew by over 25% between 1780 and 1830, but wages rose less than 5%.[25] The difference was pocketed as profits by greedy capitalists. It was this paradox of economic growth (i.e. social injustice), which prompted Friedrich Engels and Karl Marx to pen *The Communist Manifesto*. But of course, after a century of failed social experiments, we do not want to resurrect the spectre of a command-and-control economy. So what is to be done to curb the worst excesses of capitalism?

Restoring Humanity

We have already stated our belief that human nature is generally quite kind. So why is it that these fund managers, business leaders, and investment bankers — most of whom are upright citizens in their private lives — act without scruples at work? In our view, the fundamental issue seems to be the culture of hyper-competition (along with occasional backstabbing) which makes it all but impossible for us to be ourselves or trust one another. The situation is not unlike the fictional "Hunger Games," in which the selected participants must fight one another to death until only one winner is left standing. In the novel, the hero confides his feelings to the heroine (the narrator) the night before the competition:

> "I don't know how to say it exactly. Only... I want to die as myself. Does that make any sense?" he asks. I shake my head. How could he die as anyone but himself? "I don't want them to change me in there. Turn me into some kind of monster that I'm not".[26]

Here the protagonist indicates that he does not expect to win the competition. There are 24 participants, and only one can emerge alive. Rather, his goal is to maintain his decency and die as a human being. That will be his moral victory against those who have forced him to take part in this humiliating televised battle. As the plot progresses, it becomes clear that staying true to oneself is the ultimate test of character in the story.

In a competitive environment, where you are under constant pressure to outdo your peers and deliver short-term results, just staying who you are becomes a challenge. Sooner or later your heart grows hardened, and your sensitivity is dulled. This is the state which Confucians called *bu-ren*, the negative form of *ren* denoting numbness of the heart. As Cheng Hao (AD 1032–1085), a Neo-Confucian philosopher, describes it:

> In medical books, paralysis in limbs is called *bu-ren*. The expression is quite apt... [because] in such a state, even though the pain is in one's own hands and feet, one cannot perceive it as one's own pain, nor feel anything in one's heart.[27]

A man who has lost *ren* is like a paralyzed person. He no longer responds to his own pain, let alone those of others around him. He says things not because he wants to say them, but because they are what others want to hear. He does things not because he wants to do them, but because they are what is expected of him. He just reacts to market signals, without thinking too hard about the moral implications of his actions, because he needs the money and promotion. Li Zhuowu (AD 1527–1602), a radical Confucian, compares it to the loss of "a child's heart":

> When one loses a child's heart, one loses his true heart. When one loses his true heart, one loses his true humanity... [When his true humanity is lost] what one says is what he heard from others or what passes for truths, not what his child's heart produces. Although the words might be elaborate, they have nothing to do with who he is... When a fake man utters fake words, other fake men delight.[28]

Li Zhuowu knew firsthand how difficult it is to stay true to oneself in a decadent world. According to his own account, Li struggled to support his family as a low-level bureaucrat with a meager salary, yet he stubbornly refused to take bribes. One day, he came home from a long trip, only to discover that his two daughters had died from hunger. It took him a while to recover from the shock and grief, but the tragedy somehow freed him from the shackles of "fake" social obligations. He went on to quit the civil service and to write two controversial works, which he respectively called *A Book to be*

Hidden and *A Book to be Burned*. When the authorities arrested him for promulgating dangerous ideas, he cut his throat in prison, as a final form of protest against the dehumanizing forces of society.

Our conclusion is a simple one: to restore morality to our businesses, we must start by recovering our ability to feel, namely *ren*. As Jonah Lehrer, a writer on psychology, points out, the worst criminal is not someone who lacks moral reasoning but someone who feels unmoved by others' suffering — the very definition of a psychopath.[29] For the purpose of illustration, think of the recent phone hacking scandal in the UK: reporters at the *News of the World* illegally accessed the phones not only of celebrities and political figures, but of the murdered schoolgirl Milly Dowler, relatives of deceased British soldiers, and victims of the 2005 London Bombings.[30] Legal issues aside, what truly shocked the public was the astonishing lack of sensitivity. Apparently, the competition among British tabloids was so fierce that journalists working in the organization had all but lost their human sensibilities — a state which Confucians have called *bu-ren*, or numbness of the heart.

To repeat: it is our ability to feel (*ren*) which constitutes the basis of our morality. We are not alone in thinking this way. Years before the publication of *The Wealth of Nations*, Adam Smith wrote *The Theory of Moral Sentiments*, with a view to providing capitalism with the necessary moral foundation. As David Brooks points out, "Smith believed that the economic activity described in *The Wealth of Nations* rested upon the bedrock described in *The Theory of Moral Sentiments*".[31] Unfortunately, most people nowadays know about the former but not the latter. What was the basis of our moral sentiments, according to Smith? He called it "sympathy," our inborn ability to imagine what others feel:

> How selfish soever man may be supposed, there are evidently some principles in his nature, which interest him in the fortunes of others, and render their happiness necessary to him, though he derives nothing from it, except the pleasure of seeing it. Of this kind is pity or compassion, the emotion we feel for the misery of others, when we either see it, or are made to conceive it in a very lively manner.[32]

Smith believed that such sympathetic sentiments would naturally lead us to hold back our selfish desires and act benevolently toward others. We heartily agree, but want to add that hyper-competition in a capitalist society can easily paralyze our sensitivity and rob us of basic human qualities. So how do we go about restoring them?

Profit Motive as Secondary

What drives competition in a capitalist society? The answer is, of course, money. Governments compete for GDP figures; corporations, for profit; individuals, for wealth. That is the easy answer, but allow us to provide a more philosophical one: the motivation underlying various types of competition is our tendency to maximize self-interest, which economists refer to as the "profit motive." Confucians just called it "profit" (*li*) and regarded it as the opposite of *ren*. In the Confucian view *li* is like a lawless intruder who tramples upon *ren*, willfully sacrificing others' interests for the sake of maximizing one's own freedom and pleasure. That is why, in order to restore humanity (*ren*) to capitalism, we must address the issue of the profit motive (*li*). In this section, we will first see how the concept has been applied at the corporate level, and then deduce from it a general lesson for society.

Recall the two contrasting models of human nature we introduced earlier: one based on rational self-interest and the other based on *ren*. We have already examined how the differing views played out in the political realm. In the economic realm, the former (which assumes the worst about human nature) gave birth to the notion that the best way to control behavior is through financial incentives. A prime example of this idea is the agency theory, also known as the principal–agent problem.

The theory assumes that human beings are only interested in maximizing self-interest. This creates a problem for an employer (the principal): how does he ensure that an employee (the agent) works for the interests of the employer rather than his own, even when he is not directly being supervised? Economists had a stock answer: align the incentives between the agent and the principal. In the context of a company, it means that the CEO (the principal) sets certain management objectives, and the managers and employees (the agents) are paid according to how well they achieve those goals. But what about the CEO himself? How do his principals — namely, the shareholders — ensure that the CEO works for their benefit and not just his own? In 1990, two economists, Michael Jensen and Kevin Murphy, proposed a seemingly clever solution: in order to get the most out of an executive, shareholders should align his interests with theirs by tying his compensation to stock performance — by bestowing stock options, for example.

The result was a miraculous rise in CEO compensation. In the 1970s, American CEOs earned about 25 times the pay of an average worker. The ratio gradually rose to 40 times during the 1980s. Once the agency theory took hold, however, it ballooned out of all proportion. By 1996, the multiple reached 210 times. By 2000, a typical American CEO was making an eye-popping 500 times more than the average worker in his firm.[33] There was a problem, though: even as CEO compensation soared, business performance did not. In 1999, Kevin Murphy conceded that it is "difficult to document that the increase in stock-based incentives has led CEOs to work harder, smarter, or more in the interests of shareholders".[34] His co-author, Michael Jensen, also admitted in 2002 that stock-based compensation led CEOs to over-emphasize short-term results. In fact, countless studies have found no positive correlation whatsoever between executive pay and a company's performance.

But how can that be? Yochai Benkler gives three possible reasons. The first, which is well-known, is short-termism. When their compensation is tied to share price, CEOs focus on quarterly earnings and overlook long-term sources of value creation and sustainability. The second, more subtle reason is self-selection: companies which grant stock options tend to attract those executives who are primarily concerned with monetary rewards. The third, most pernicious reason is *cultural*: the super-sized paycheck of the CEO signals to the rest of the organization that money is everything, far exceeding effort or collaboration in terms of value. As Benkler observes, "[E]xcessively high executive salaries frame the culture of an organization as one in which it's okay to be greedy, self-serving, and uncooperative".[35] The discrepancy in compensation poisons the company culture, and the employees ultimately grow detached, resentful, and cynical. Think about it: if the managerial goal is purely economic — if, as former IBM chairman John Akers once said, the purpose of a company is to maximize the stockholders' return on equity (and thereby inflate executive pay) — how can employees identify with their organization, or feel motivated to advance the group's interests ahead of their own?[36]

Given the above, it was natural that Confucians warned about the risk of economic rationality overriding group solidarity. Specifically, they held that pursuit of profit (*li*) should not be the guiding principle of leadership, as shown in Mencius's famous exchange with King Hui of Liang:

> Mencius went to see King Hui of Liang, who said, "Sir, since you have not counted it far to come here, a distance of a thousand leagues, may I presume that you can offer counsels to profit my kingdom?" Mencius replied, "Why must your Majesty speak of profit? What I can provide are counsels to benevolence and righteousness, and they are my only topics. If your Majesty say, 'What is to be done to profit my kingdom?' the senior officers will say, 'What is to be done to profit our families?' and the inferior officers and the common people will say, 'What is to be done to profit our persons?' Superiors and inferiors will try to snatch profit from one another, and the kingdom will be endangered".[37]

Here Mencius cautions the king that if he leads his kingdom on the basis of profit-seeking, he will end up fostering a culture of selfishness and greed. People will start looking only after themselves and the kingdom will fall apart. What is the alternative? Mencius proclaims that one must lead on the principles of benevolence (*ren*) and righteousness (*yi*, also translated as social justice) instead. In the context of modern business, the first principle would mean that a leader must genuinely care about his people; the second, that the goal of a company must be something nobler than profit — say, contributing to the broader community. That way, as Francis Fukuyama points out in his book *Trust*, employees will see they are "part of something larger than themselves" and feel "a certain sense of pride" in their company.[38] Moreover, as Benkler notes, they will feel "nurtured and rewarded — not necessarily financially, but socially and intrinsically".[39]

One might ask, "But how can a company not pursue profit?" We are not saying that a company should not make a profit. As the great management guru Peter Drucker once quipped, it is hard to imagine how a bankrupt company can benefit society. Drucker further warns that although "profitability is not the purpose of business enterprise," a company must generate "sufficient profit to cover the risks of economic activity and thus to avoid loss".[40] The point we are trying to make is that the profit motive (*li*) must be *secondary* to the principles of benevolence (*ren*) and righteousness (*yi*). Otherwise, business activity degenerates into a game of cat-and-mouse, where the principal (an employer) has to be constantly on guard to catch a cheating agent (an employee). In such a situation, no loyalty or trust can exist between an employer and an employee — or between a buyer and a supplier, for that matter — as "superiors and inferiors will try to snatch profit from one another." It is hard to think of a more dehumanizing working environment.

We have said this repeatedly, but it is worth reemphasizing: we must discard rational self-interest, a.k.a. the profit motive, as the prevailing model of human nature. Not only is it dangerously simplistic, but it is actively harmful. By openly endorsing utilitarian calculation of self-interest, it condones selfishness and greed; breeds a culture of money worship; exacerbates social competition; gives rise to contentious litigation; erodes loyalty and trust; and dehumanizes us to a point where we see one another as moneymaking tools (a means) rather than as fellow human beings (an end in itself). This may sound like dull moralizing, but the truth is that a society which prizes profit-making above all else is destined to decay sooner or later. The *Great Learning*, a Confucian classic from the Warring States period, ends with this astute observation, which was meant for the rulers of ancient states but still rings true today:

If a leader makes profit-making his chief business, he will end up employ-ing the services of greedy men. His intentions may be good, but when such small men control the affairs, calamities from Heaven and injuries from men will befall the state... This is why a true leader must not consider profit-making his profit, but regard enacting righteousness as his profit.[41]

Challenges for China

If you think we are exaggerating the dangers of the unbridled pursuit of profit, look no further than what is happening in China. China today suffers from all of the problems of capitalism mentioned thus far, only more acutely: money worship, excessive competition, ram-pant social injustice, a breakdown in morality, and a deficit of social trust. While the problems are multifold and interrelated, here we will highlight two issues in particular: product safety and labor conditions.

1. Product safety

In *The Theory of Moral Sentiments*, Adam Smith emphasizes the importance of the "impartial spectator" in all of us, which he defines as "reason, principle, conscience, the inhabitant of the breast, the man within, the great judge and arbiter of our conduct"[42] — in short, our inner sense of right and wrong. Even in the supposedly self-correcting capitalist system, the morality of the participants matters. In fact, it is frightening to think of what happens when businessmen, blinded by the pursuit of profit, casually ignore their conscience.

In 2007, *The New York Times* ran a long exposé of the deadly poi-soning which killed at least 145 patients at Panama City's public hospital. At first, doctors could not figure out what was happening. The patients exhibited unusual symptoms, starting as a weakness or tingling sensation in their legs which then spread upward to cause paralysis and an inability to breathe. They also lost the ability to urinate. The death rate from the mystery illness approached 50%, and many of the survivors were condemned to endure devastating paralysis for the rest of their lives. When a special task force looked into the situation, they discovered that all of the patients had been given the same cough medicine. Lab tests of the medicine by the US Centers for Disease Control and Prevention turned up diethylene glycol, a deadly chemical which had been used in place of glycerine. The ingredient originated from a manufacturer called the Taixing Glycerine Factory in China. The toxic syrup was labeled "99.5 percent pure glycerine," although the factory was not even certified to make pharmaceutical ingredients.[43] It then passed through middlemen in Beijing and Barcelona before ending up in Panama.

Unsurprisingly, it is the Chinese themselves who suffer the most from the unethical behavior of their merchants. Shortly before the Panama case broke out, one of the finest hospitals in Guangdong saw scores of patients die from a medicine for treating gall bladder problems. The cause was traced back to a man named Wang, "a tailor with a ninth-grade education and access to a chemistry book".[44] Wang found a reference to diethylene glycol in his chemistry book and realized he could make easy money by selling it to the drug industry. The final death count from his misdeed remains unclear, but it was obviously not an isolated case, as evidenced by Premier Wen Jiabao's pronouncement shortly thereafter that "the pharmaceutical market is in disorder".[45] Nor is the drug industry alone in suffering contamination in its supply chain — remember the Sanlu baby milk scandal? Food safety has been a chronic concern. Yanzhong Huang, a senior fellow for global health at the Council on Foreign Relations, enumerates the cases of "meat containing the banned steroid clenbuterol, rice contaminated with cadmium, noodles flavored with ink and paraffin, mushrooms treated with fluorescent bleach and cooking oil recycled from street gutters".[46]

Another worry is the safety of buildings and infrastructure, as the recent train collision in Wenzhou shows. In July 2011, China saw not one but *three* bridges collapse, injuring scores of drivers and passengers. The year before, a bridge collapse in Henan province claimed 37 lives. The shoddy quality of the construction was blamed on corrupt local officials. For example, *The China Daily* reported in 2007 that an official was given a life sentence for taking bribes during the bidding process for construction of the Qianjiang bridge in Hangzhou — one of the three bridges which broke down in July

2011.[47] Combine these sorts of risk with the pervasive problems of air quality and water safety, and it is not an exaggeration to say that life in China today is never really safe, no matter how rich and privileged one may be.

2. Labor conditions

Alexandra Harney, who for a long time has covered China for the *Financial Times*, called her recent book *The China Price*. The title has a dual meaning. The popular meaning of the China price is the incredibly cheap prices of consumer goods — these days one can buy a T-shirt for $3 and a DVD player for $30 — which has been made possible by the low-cost labor of China. The second meaning, which is the real meaning of her book, refers to the true price China has to pay — social, human, and environmental costs — in order for its firms to maintain their competitive edge. Going through the book is like reading a modern-day rendition of *Les Misérables*, except the happy ending has yet to be written.

By far, the biggest success story of China has been the offshore manufacturing boom, which propelled the country to overtake America as the largest manufacturer in the world. The success came at a cost, though. Harney recounts the example of a worker named Deng, who found a job at a small gemstone factory in Guangdong in 1997. The factory processed the quartz, onyx, and carnelian used in costumes and ornaments, which were then exported to the US and South America. Harney remarks, "The products may have been pretty, but there was nothing glamorous about their work".[48] Deng worked 12-hour shifts, seven days a week, for a take-home pay of less than $200 a month — which was considered high back then. Workers could be fined for the most trivial "offences," such as taking a day off. Most importantly, permanently sealed windows held in the dusty air in the gem drilling section where Deng worked.

In the summer of 2000, Deng developed deep and persistent cough. He was diagnosed with silicosis, a deadly lung disease caused by the inhalation of crystalline silica dust. Five other colleagues developed similar symptoms and were immediately hospitalized. When Deng and his colleagues were released from the hospital about a month later, the factory promptly discharged them.[49] Deng's wife, who was working in the same factory, was also fired without compensation. As Deng's health deteriorated, the couple fell deeply into debt, but they continued fighting their former employer for compensation. They finally won the case in 2005, when the court awarded them about $30,000, but most of the money was used to repay creditors. Deng passed away shortly thereafter, at the age of 36.

Unfortunately, this kind of tragedy is far too common. Harney cites a UNDP report which estimates that over 200 million workers in China are exposed to dangerous working conditions. According to the Xinhua News Agency, China had 665,043 recorded cases of occupational illness in 2005, with 606,891 cases classified as "pneumoconiosis," an umbrella term which includes "black lung" for coal miners as well as silicosis. And that is just official reporting; the actual incidence is probably much higher.[50] To put it bluntly, human life in China has a price nowadays. The going rate is reportedly 250,000 yuan, or about $40,000, as judged by compensation awards for workers killed at a construction site.[51]

Workplace safety is just one of many issues facing Chinese workers today. In another heartbreaking example cited by Harney, a bright young man named Li persevered through appalling working conditions — 18 hours a day, 7 days a week, for a monthly salary of $39 and an apartment shared with seven or eight other workers — just so that he could earn money to go back to school.[52] His dream was abruptly shattered when he lost his right hand and half of his forearm in an industrial accident. It is unclear whether the accident was caused by his own slip-up, but even if it was, how can anyone blame him for negligence when he was working 126 hours a week? He could have been too tired to concentrate; the accident happened late at night. Sadly, this kind of sweatshop conditions is quite standard for migrant workers from the countryside. Most of them are not entitled to legal protection or a social safety net under the country's notorious household registration (hukou) system. (The Chinese government, to its credit, has extended health insurance coverage to most workers in recent years — albeit under a plan which discriminates between "urban workers" and "rural workers."[53])

Multiple parties are to blame for this state of affairs. The central government has put in place stringent labor laws — the legal limit for working hours (including overtime) is 204 hours per month, or less than 50 hours per week[54] — but local governments, in their eagerness to rack up economic growth, do not enforce them. Western buyers also bear blame for paying lip service to workers' rights, but then (knowingly) demanding impossibly low prices, tight delivery deadlines, or both. Then of course there are the factory owners, who have no qualms about breaking labor laws, bribing government-appointed inspectors, or forging fake time cards to show to the auditors. As one factory owner tells it, "Everyone knows that everyone cheats... Everyone knows this is only the rules of the game".[55]

Suggestions for a Humane Economy

The examples here serve to show that China must rectify the way it practices capitalism, the so-called "China model" of growth. So what kinds of reforms should the country undertake? Western economists offer a stock prescription: China should become a truly capitalist economy, unburdened by state influence. However, as we hope readers will agree by now, further liberalization of the economy — "more markets, competition, and freedom for enterprise, including state-owned companies"[56] — will likely aggravate, rather than ameliorate, the myriad social ills of China. What ails China is not the lack of free enterprise; if anything, the country may have too much of it. The real problem is the culture of excessive profit-seeking (*li*) which pervades all levels of society.

The single-minded pursuit of profit is a dangerous phenomenon which can dull our sensitivities and gradually obliterate all other social and human considerations. While Confucians did not deny the validity of the profit motive *per se*, they held that it should be brought under control by a spirit of benevolence and righteousness. Based on this broad principle, let us now make pragmatic suggestions for building a humane economy at the state, corporate, and individual levels.

1. Economic security over GDP growth (state level)

The key to China's stellar growth is the ferocious competition among provinces, cities, and counties. Here is how it functions: each locality has a party secretary, who has near-dictatorial powers within his jurisdiction. Each party secretary uses those overwhelming powers to attract investment, build infrastructure, and invest in local companies, so that his locality may report a faster growth rate than its neighbours. Beijing actively incentivizes such competition, and the winners are rewarded with promotion within the party system.

But things can go too far. According to *The Economist*, Beijing encouraged banks to relax lending in response to the global financial crisis. China's banks increased their loan books by almost $1.5 trillion (twice the size of the Indian banking system) in 2009 alone. Much of that money flowed into 10,000 or so "investment companies" owned by local governments, which financed "roads, bridges, irrigation works and some housing schemes of dubious merit".[57] Such white-elephant projects may add a few percentage points to GDP growth in the short term, but many of them will fail to raise enough revenue to repay the loan. This kind of investment-led growth is hardly sustainable. Already the share of investment spending in China's economy has reached almost half of the GDP, much of it driven by the boom in real estate and construction. What we are witnessing may be a time bomb, a new danger spot in the world economy which doesn't need another one.

Aside from the macroeconomic imbalances, the obsession with growth has created social imbalances, as shown by the extreme level of inequality and the continued lack of worker protections. It has also exacerbated environmental degradation, as local bureaucrats routinely turn a blind eye to polluting industries. The most damaging effect may be cultural though, as it encourages too many people to behave as if anything can be justified for the sake of making money. Corruption is not restricted to bureaucrats anymore; it is everywhere, as noted by Nicholas Kristof, a *New York Times* columnist:

> Even good people are on the take in China these days, because everybody
> else is. Chinese doctors take cash from patients' families before surgery.
> Journalists take bribes to write articles. Principals take money to admit stu-
> dents… One Chinese friend of mine was a judge in corruption cases, and
> made a good living taking bribes from defendants.[58]

We have said earlier that a society which prizes profit-making above all else is bound to decay sooner or later; here we have living proof. In another shocking revelation, the state media reported that a railways official had managed to steal a staggering $2.8 billion and move it abroad.[59] More recently, *The New York Times* caused a stir when it reported that the relatives of Wen Jiabao, the outgoing premier, had also accumulated wealth of $2.7 billion.[60] How many more warning signs does Beijing need? Our contention is that the relentless pursuit of wealth (*li*) at the national level is largely responsible for the stunning collapse of values. The party leadership should break out of its addiction to growth, before things really get out of hand.

So what should replace GDP growth as the goal of macroeconomic policy? Mencius says that a compassionate government has three policy objectives: providing for the least advantaged ("widows, widowers, solitary seniors, and orphans… who have none whom they can lean on"[61]); mitigating economic volatility ("an intelligent ruler will regulate the livelihood of the people, so that… in bad years they shall escape the danger of perishing"[62]); and ensuring that everyone has job security ("a constant means of production," also translated as "a reliable livelihood"[63]). In other words, what Mencius calls for is economic security. In the modern context, the appropriate policy response would involve such things as universal healthcare, a national pension system, unemployment benefits, affordable public housing, and assisted childcare — in short, institutions which help the society bear risks together.

2. Employees over shareholders (corporate level)

The management–labor relations in China are among the most hostile in the world. We have already noted how factory owners regularly expose their workers to harsh and unsafe working conditions.

Not surprisingly, employees are not particularly loyal to their employers. In a Chinese factory, it is common for 20%–30% of the migrant workers to disappear after a long break in the Chinese New Year, without even notifying the management. Employers have responded by requiring deposits from new hires and withholding salary payments. The trust level between workers and management is close to nil, and the supplier–buyer relationship is just as fraught with mistrust.

The current situation poses a challenge for China if its economy is to transition from cheap manufacturing to more value-added industries. Employers are not willing to invest in worker training when their workers might switch jobs for the slightest pay differential. Employees are not motivated to innovate or deliver good services when they believe the employers will pocket all the rewards. The result is that many Chinese firms struggle to differentiate themselves in the overcrowded market, and too often they compete only on the basis of cost.

For a viable alternative, China should look to Japan as a model. Although Japan Inc. is going through a rough patch at the moment, historically its firms have been exceptional when it comes to building harmonious labor relations. The best example may well be the Toyota-GM plant in Fremont, California, which was formerly run by Toyota's management. Instead of monitoring employees' every move (à la the "scientific management" pioneered by Frederick Taylor), Toyota emphasized autonomy and collaboration. Team members and managers were treated as equal partners, with managers soliciting input from even the lowest-ranking employees. As Yochai Benkler observes, "[B]y trusting its employees in a way that none of its American counterparts would dream of, Toyota built an unprecedented level of employee engagement and trust in return".[64] Toyota also reshaped the supplier–buyer relationship by applying the same trusting approach to its suppliers. Instead of squeezing every penny, Toyota worked together with its suppliers on quality improvements and built long-term partnerships.

The result is now legendary. When Toyota took over the management of the Fremont plant in 1982, its workforce was considered "the worst workforce in the automobile industry in the United States" by the United Auto Workers.[65] By the end of 1984, however, the revamped plant "surpassed any other GM plant in productivity and had the highest-quality ranking of any automobile plant in the United States".[66] Benkler notes that the Toyota approach reflects a fundamentally benign view of human nature. The "scientific management" approach assumes the worst about human nature, and it controls employees' behavior through close supervision and financial incentives. What the Japanese realized instead was that most employees could be intrinsically motivated only if they fostered "an inclusive, social, and collaborative workplace".[67]

That also meant having relatively equal salaries. In an organization where the guiding principles were fairness and cooperation, "there was less need for, or justification of, ridiculously inflated wages".[68] The consequence for the wider society is that although Japan does not have the kind of redistributive policies that Europe does, it enjoys one of the lowest income inequalities among industrialized nations. As Richard Wilkinson and Kate Picket observe in *The Spirit Level: Why Greater Equality Makes Societies Stronger*,

> As a proportion of national income, public social expenditure in Japan is, in contrast to Sweden, among the lowest of the major developed countries. Japan gets its high degree of equality not so much from redistribution as from a greater equality of market incomes, of earnings *before* taxes and benefits.[69]

The Japanese government can take a hands-off approach to inequality, because pre-tax income distribution is relatively equal to start with. (In fact, it is another Confucian society, South Korea, which enjoys the greatest equality of pre-tax income among developed nations.[70]) The combination of a small government and low inequality sounds wonderful, doesn't it? Japan developed its unique corporate culture due to its tradition of *bushido*, the Way of the Warrior-Knight, which in turn grew out of Neo-Confucianism during the Tokugawa era. The key tenet of *bushido* is righteousness (*yi*, pronounced *gi* in Japanese), a concept promulgated by Mencius: "There should be righteousness between a ruler and a subject".[71] A ruler could not expect loyalty and sacrifice from his knights if he was seen as greedy and self-serving — i.e. lacking in *yi*. For this reason, modern-day CEOs in Japan are careful not to pay themselves lavishly, in stark contrast to their American peers. (Using 2004–2006 data, American CEOs at top corporations made on average $13.3 million a year, while their Japanese counterparts at comparable firms only received $1.5 million.[72])

And these Japanese CEOs actually care about their employees. Management theorist Koji Sakamoto says that a company has five stakeholders — employees, suppliers, customers, community, and shareholders — with employees being the most important.[73] Why does he place employees above even the customers? The reason is because a company cannot create great products or deliver exceptional services with disgruntled employees. Creating happy customers starts with happy employees. This line of thinking is consistent with what many business owners and managers preach and practice in Japan, despite the Western concept of "shareholder capitalism" which has unfortunately made inroads during the last two decades. After the scandals at Enron, WorldCom, Tyco International, Global Crossing, and Adelphia, we don't think we need to elaborate the harmful effects of shareholder capitalism. Suffice it to say that Jack Welch of General Electric, who coined the expression in the first place, later disavowed it, calling it "the dumbest idea in the world".[74]

3. Social realization over money (individual level)

We began this chapter by noting the key difference between Taoism and Confucianism, which we framed as *laissez-faire* versus social realization. In practice, what the former meant was that Taoists stayed away from worldly affairs. Many Taoist philosophers were hermits who had withdrawn from the secular world of politics. Confucians, on the other hand, regarded joining the civil service as an essential means of social realization. For instance, there is a scene in the *Analects* where a Taoist recluse criticizes Confucius for dabbling in politics instead of getting a real job (farming).[75] A disciple defends his master by saying that while social ideals are difficult to realize, one must not give up trying. Basically the Taoist position can be summed up as, "Go with the flow. Don't bother to change the world." The Confucian reply was, "If someone doesn't try, how can we realize social justice?"

Fortunately, one does not have to enter the government to bring about social changes nowadays. An entrepreneur can contribute to the world as much as any policymaker by pushing the frontier of technology or providing quality products at affordable prices. In the same vein, John Bogle makes a distinction between a capitalist and an entrepreneur. By his definition, a capitalist is someone who will do anything for profit. An entrepreneur, in contrast, is someone like Benjamin Franklin, who created numerous inventions and enterprises "for the public weal, not for his personal profit".[76] For example, Franklin created America's first fire insurance company, but he did not financially benefit from it because it was organized as a mutual insurance company. As Bogle notes,

> He also founded a library, an academy and college, a hospital, and a learned society — none for his personal enrichment, all for the benefit of his community... Like many entrepreneurs, Franklin was also an inventor... Among other devices, he created the lightning rod and the Franklin stove (to say nothing of bifocals and swim fins). He made no attempt to patent the lightning rod for his own profit, and he declined the offer by the governor of the Commonwealth for a patent on his Franklin stove...[77]

Bogle contrasts Franklin's noble conduct with the bitter patent wars and obscene executive pay of today, concluding that "the differences verge on the appalling".[78] We hope the new generation of entrepreneurs will look toward not just Steve Jobs — whose fine reputation was unfortunately tainted by an options backdating scandal and patent-infringement lawsuits — but Benjamin Franklin as a role model. As hard as it is, they should aspire to achieve more with their lives than just making money.

Christianity, Communism, and Claims of Community

China is one of the five surviving communist countries in the world (the other four being North Korea, Vietnam, Laos, and Cuba). As its constitution unequivocally states, "The guiding ideology of the People's Republic of China is Marxism-Leninism-Mao Zedong Thought".[79] But China today is nothing like a communist society. The country is a more unequal society than even the US or Russia, and it boasts more billionaires than any other country except the US.[80] Aside from the Leninist dictatorship, its socioeconomic system is now so far removed from communism that some people refer to it as "party-state capitalism." It is a little known fact, but the Chinese Communist Party seriously considered jettisoning the word "Communist" from its name in the early 2000s.[81] Pragmatism prevailed in the end, with the party deciding that a name change would be too disruptive. What the episode shows, though, is that the party has all but lost its aspiration to build a classless society, which is its stated purpose of existence. Given the situation, it is worthwhile to reflect on what communism means for China today.

It may come as a surprise, but historically the precursors to Marxism came primarily from the ranks of Christian clergymen. Although Jesus never explicitly denied ownership of property, his teachings occasionally exhibited anti-capitalist sentiments, e.g. "It is easier for a camel to go through the eye of a needle than for a rich man to enter the kingdom of God" (Matthew 19:24). According to Archie Brown, an acclaimed historian of communism, such teachings led early Christians to uphold common possession as an ideal. For instance, Saint Ambrose of Milan wrote in the 4th century, "Nature has poured forth all things for all men, to be held in common."[82] During medieval times, John Wycliffe, an English theologian, held that "all good things of God ought to be held in common," and John Ball, a preacher who took part in the Peasants' Revolt of 1381, declared that "[t]hings cannot go well in England... until all goods are held in common".[83] The finest early portrayal of the communist ideal is to be found, of course, in Saint Thomas More's *Utopia*, in which the narrator declares, "I'm quite convinced that you'll never get a fair distribution of goods, or a satisfactory organization of human life, until you abolish private property altogether".[84]

The more unfortunate aspect of Christianity which inspired communism was its eschatology, the belief in an imminent apocalypse — a showdown between good and evil — to be followed by a millennium of heaven on earth. The Millennial philosophy inspired Karl Marx to dream of the day the proletariat would overthrow the capitalists through a class war. As Bertrand Russell observes, one can easily reconstruct Marx's psychology as follows[85] :

Judeo-Christianity	*Marxism*
Yahweh	Dialectical Materialism
The Messiah	Marx
The Elect	The Proletariat
The Church	The Communist Party
The Second Coming	The Revolution
Hell	Punishment of the Capitalists
The Millennium	The Communist Commonwealth

Whether Jesus himself subscribed to the Millennial vision is questionable. Albert Schweitzer famously portrayed the historical Jesus as an "apocalyptic prophet," but we doubt that Jesus saw himself that way. For instance, the *Gospel of Thomas*, which predates the Canonical Gospels, does not make a single mention of the apocalypse. It is more likely that Jesus believed salvation could be obtained at a personal level through introspection and that he viewed himself as a source of inspiration and guidance toward that end. The core messages he repeats time and again are those of loving, sharing, and forgiving — in short, salvation from within, not salvation from without. Although he clashed with the oppressive rulers and hypocritical rabbis of his time, the revolution he sought was of a spiritual kind, not a political kind.

In contrast, Marx was an impatient messiah who sought to realize heaven on earth by upending the capitalist order. His motivation may have been pure — as mentioned, it was the Dickensian poverty of workers in England which drove Marx and Engels to write *The Communist Manifesto* — but his vision was too simplistic, his methods too radical. That was his biggest departure from the teachings of

Jesus, who taught us to forgive our enemies, not to overthrow them by violent means.

So what shall we make of the communist experiment, which at one point controlled one-third of the human race? The most obvious lesson is that communal ownership does not work. Not only does it sap individuals of motivation, but people have realized that life is quite dull and colourless without markets — a bit like those faded monochrome photographs from the Soviet days. Markets serve as an essential conduit for realizing human desires. Although markets are full of fights, frauds, and contradictions, they also provide our lives with joys, heartbreaks, and dramas.

In fact, market-based capitalism has existed since time immemorial, long before Adam Smith came along. It is the most *natural* form of economic organization — as opposed to communal ownership, which has been the *ideal* of social reformers through the ages. One may argue that capitalism is the *sein* (what is) of human society, while communism is its *sollen* (what should be). Confucians explicitly denounced equality based on communal ownership because, in the end, it was just too unnatural.[86]

Still, Marx's heart was in the right place, based as it were on the Christian ethos of loving and sharing. That was why so many intellectuals of the 20th century fell for his vision of a workers' utopia, even though his proposed means to get there was wrongheaded. To the extent that the communist movement forced Western democracies to adopt better worker protections and social safety nets, one could even argue that it *saved* capitalism from its own worst excesses in the 20th century.

Our suggestion is for the Chinese Communist Party to retain the humanitarian aspirations of communism, but to drop its revolutionary mission which has its origin in the Millennial Christianity. And it should no longer enshrine Marx and Lenin in its constitution. As we have seen, the communist philosophy itself existed long before Marx and Lenin, and it must be opened up to creative reinvention and amelioration. One idea is to reinterpret communism as a kind of communitarianism. Modern communitarian philosophy has risen as a reaction against the liberal conception of individual freedom. Its proponents, notably Alasdair MacIntyre and Michael Sandel, point out that individuals are not free, independent beings who exist in a vacuum; rather, we are all "encumbered selves" who are bound by "obligations of solidarity and loyalty, historic memory and religious faith — moral claims that arise from the communities and traditions that shape our identity".[87] In other words, our group identity matters at least as much as our individual identity, and this has far-reaching implications on how we think of issues such as economic freedom and property rights. A self-made billionaire may claim that his wealth is all due to his own genius and labor, but then where did his advantages come from, if not from the society he was born into? We conclude this discussion with a speech given by Elizabeth Warren during her recent senate campaign, which makes a compelling case for "claims of community" — and crushes neoliberal orthodoxy along the way:

> I hear all this, you know, "Well, this is class warfare, this is whatever." No! There is nobody in this country who got rich on his own. Nobody. You built a factory out there — good for you! But I want to be clear. You moved your goods to market on the roads the rest of us paid for. You hired workers the rest of us paid to educate. You were safe in your factory because of police forces and fire forces that the rest of us paid for. You didn't have to worry that marauding bands would come and seize everything at your factory, and hire someone to protect against this, because of the work the rest of us did. Now look, you built a factory and it turned into something terrific, or a great idea — God bless. Keep a big hunk of it. But part of the underlying social contract is you take a hunk of that and pay forward for the next kid who comes along.[88]

* * *

Confucianism was unabashedly pro-market. Confucius regarded the tithe (a 10% tax) as an ideal tax law, because it did not unduly burden the private sector which was the driving force of a prosperous economy.[89] In another example, Wang Anshi, a Neo-Confucian scholar best known for his political reforms, slashed taxes on farmers and merchants in order to stimulate the economy — and made up for the shortfall by making collection fairer. Wang Anshi, in turn, drew his inspiration from Mencius, who advocated using the effective tax rate of one-ninth (11.1%) for farmers and abolishing levies altogether for traveling merchants.[90] What these examples clearly show is that Confucians appreciated the power of markets to make a nation flourish and to enrich people's lives.

Even so, Confucians were well aware of the pitfalls of free markets, and they warned against the danger of economic rationality running roughshod over social and human considerations. Their proposed remedy, again, was cultural rather than institutional. This is both the weakness and the strength of Confucianism. On one hand, Confucianism never produced the modern concepts of the welfare state, labour rights, and corporate governance. On the other hand, it does offer highly pragmatic insights for instilling the right capitalist culture and cultivating the right kind of business leaders. And what we need more of right now is the latter.

Just as in the realm of politics, the limits of purely institution-based economic reforms are becoming clear. European-style welfare states are becoming harder to sustain because of the "race to the bottom" among nations to offer lower taxes and lighter regulation. As Jeffrey Sachs notes, even within the US, "[t]he fifty states are in competition with one another for businesses and wealthy citizens. By keeping tax rates just a bit lower than others, each state can attract business and revenues".[91] The obvious result is that almost all states are now starved for cash, but no state will dare propose a tax hike unilaterally, because its businesses would then threaten to move elsewhere.

Meanwhile, multinational corporations and wealthy individuals are getting ever better at dodging taxes and bypassing regulations, and they seem to have no qualms about enriching themselves at society's expense. Unfortunately, when it comes to inducing the private sector to act more responsibly, the proposed measures appear insipid and toothless. Has the "balanced scorecard" made corporations fairer in their dealings with various stakeholders? Has the Corporate Social Responsibility (CSR), with its triple bottom-line reporting, made executives take social and ecological issues more seriously? Will the proposed "Tobin Tax" on financial transactions dissuade speculators from wilfully rocking the currency markets? Not really. Institutional remedies will help, but given the pervasive and deep-rooted nature of the problems, we suspect that nothing short of a fundamental transformation in culture can correct the course of capitalism.

Chapter

4

On Education

If another person succeeds by one effort, try it a hundred times. If another person succeeds by ten practices, practice it a thousand times. If one proceeds this way, even the dull will surely become wise, and even the weak will surely become strong.

Doctrine of the Mean, Chapter 20

Educational Arms Race

In the preceding chapter, we saw that education is a principal source of economic hardship for the middle class. Competition for higher educational credentials is growing ever fiercer, unduly burdening family finances everywhere. To take the US as an example, it is not just skyrocketing college tuitions which are putting families in a bind. Many parents feel they have no choice but to take on unaffordable mortgages, because public schools at both the elementary and secondary levels are assigned by zip codes. As Elizabeth Warren notes, when middle-class parents purchase expensive suburban homes, they are really "buying education" because too often it is the only way their children can attend decent public schools. The consequence is that couples with children are more than twice as likely to go broke as their childless counterparts. In fact, having a child is now the "single best predictor" of personal bankruptcy.[1]

What this situation means is that there may be no easy solution to the financial predicament of the middle class. Suppose the US adopted the European model and used the power of the state to redistribute wealth. Most of the middle class would be better off as a result. But would higher income really solve their problems? Many people would reply yes. According to Derek Bok, the former president of Harvard University, Americans on average say that if only they made $90,000 more per year, they could "fulfill all their dreams".[2] We suspect they are wrong, though. Imagine what would happen if the median household income suddenly doubled, thanks to a radical redistributive policy. Would the middle class feel more secure? Well, we already have people making that level of income, who are called the upper-middle class. See how David Brooks describes them in *The Social Animal*:

> ...they all have to deal with the emotional consequences of their Sublimated Liquidity Rage, which is the anger felt by Upper-Middle Class Americans who make decent salaries but have to spend 60 percent of their disposable incomes on private-school tuitions. They have nothing left to spend on themselves, which causes deep and unacknowledged self-pity.[3]

Brooks is obviously being facetious, but the insight here is worth noting: the upper-middle class is also feeling squeezed, because of the pressure to give their children the best possible education. While the middle class is under strain, the upper-middle class is also struggling to pay for overpriced private schools.

Here is what we believe would happen if America adopted a purely redistributive policy, with no accompanying reform in its public education system: the middle class would experience temporary relief, as they use their higher income to pay off debt and build up savings. In the long run, however, housing prices in good neighborhoods and private-school tuitions would also rise across the board, offsetting much of the gain. Higher income is not the panacea which some make it out to be, because the educational arms race is the real culprit behind the plight of the middle class. Just as in the military arms race, investment in education by one party tends to offset the investment of another, making everyone worse off. As Ha-Joon Chang wryly notes:

> The higher education system… is like a theatre in which some people decided to stand to get a better view, prompting others behind them to stand. Once enough people stand, everyone has to stand, which means no one is getting a better view, while everyone has become more uncomfortable.[4]

To be fair, competition for higher education is not exactly a zero-sum game, as it does raise the educational standard of the overall population. However, it is also highly wasteful from a societal viewpoint, because parents have a tendency to overinvest in the educational credentials of their children. They essentially have no choice, since most employers use degrees as an initial screening tool. Once every student has a high school diploma, one needs a college degree to stand out in the job market. Once every student has a college degree, a master's or even a PhD is needed. And so on. The result is misery all around, as parents struggle to pay tuition and/or students find themselves saddled with unmanageable debt upon graduation.

Money, Education, and the Democratic Ideal

Why is it, then, that this destructive competition shows no sign of abating? The reason is, of course, economic. As Charles Murray categorically states, "[B]rains became much more valuable in the marketplace".[5] Evidence bears him out. According to a study by Ron Haskins and Isabel Sawhill of the Brookings Institution, nowadays a typical high-school dropout in America belongs to a family making $28,000 a year; the median high-school graduate, $42,000; the median college graduate, $75,000; and the median American with a graduate degree, $93,000.[6] Inequality is even more pronounced at the high end. An analysis by Murray shows that close to half of the graduates from America's top universities (Harvard, Yale, and Princeton) live in what he calls "SuperZips," the cushy neighborhoods which fall within the top five percentile in income and education levels, with median family income of $141,400.[7] It is as if "the college sorting machine replicates itself with remarkable fidelity as a residential sorting machine".[8] The surest way to join this new upper class is to attend an elite university — a fact which underlies the intensity of competition for admission to such schools.

One might ask, "But what is wrong with that?" A capitalist economy should reward those who are talented and hard-working. Assuming the graduates of elite schools are indeed brighter and more disciplined than their peers, is it not natural that they make more money — especially in a knowledge-driven economy where their exceptional cognitive ability can add greater value? This might be a legitimate question if everyone had equal access to higher education. Unfortunately, the college admission process in the US is hardly fair. Joseph Soares, author of *The Power of Privilege*, points out that 79% of students at Tier 1 colleges came from the top quartile of socioeconomic status during the 1990s, whereas only 2% were from the bottom quartile.[9] If we also consider that college tuition has spiked in recent years — in the US, the average sticker price for attending a private college for one year was $42,224 in 2011[10] — it becomes clear that higher education is not the agent of social mobility it used to be. In fact, it is now one of the chief means by which the rich perpetuate their privilege. The situation today is a stunning reversal from the progressive ideal of education as described by John Dewey in his seminal work, *Democracy and Education*, first published in 1916.

One of Dewey's objectives in writing the book was to eliminate the artificial distinction between liberal education and vocational training, which embodied class division in a pre-industrial society. Dewey traced the origin of liberal education to ancient Greece, where a small number of citizens were relieved from labor and thus free to engage in purely intellectual pursuits. The rest of population — including most women and slaves — were trained only for "useful" labor. In short, the division between the leisure and laboring classes corresponded to two modes of education: the liberal or intellectual on the one hand, and the useful or manual on the other. Such division persisted well into the 19th century, as the landed aristocrats in feudal societies also held that "practical" labor was beneath them and led "the life of observation, cogitation, and speculation" instead.[11]

By the time of Dewey, however, such distinction had become anachronistic. Landed aristocrats had long been superseded by new industrialists, a development which effectively ended serfdom and slavery. Democratic ideals were taking hold across American society, as symbolized by the achievement of women's suffrage in 1920. A common school system of education, public and free, was already well-established and expanding rapidly. No wonder, then, that Dewey sought to abolish the division between "practical" and "liberal" education, which doomed children of the working class to forever stay in the working class. He held that education has to ameliorate rather than aggravate inequality, in accordance with democratic ideals.

> ...the present industrial constitution of society is, like every society which has ever existed, full of inequities. It is the aim of progressive education to take part in correcting unfair privilege and unfair deprivation, not to perpetuate them.[12]

For Dewey, egalitarian education was the key requirement for bringing about a truly democratic society. By providing equality of opportunity, it did away with class privilege altogether. It also inculcated civic virtues into the wider population — a prerequisite if citizens were to adequately perform their public duties under a democratic system. Seen in this light, the growing link between money and education today appears even more problematic, as it has the potential to undermine the very foundation of a democratic society.

What might be done to address the equality gap in education? The immediate response should be institutional. Elizabeth Warren and Amelia Tyagi (Warren's daughter) advanced several cogent recommendations in *The Two-Income Trap*: a tuition freeze at public universities; universal preschool beginning at age 3; and school vouchers to decouple schools from home location.[13] They all appear to be sensible measures in the American context, but then they do not really address the heart of the problem: the educational arms race, which in turn is driven by the rising income differentials based on education level. Clearly, restoring confidence in public education should be the priority, as it is still the best way to ensure some degree of equality of opportunity as a society. Beyond that, however, it would be hard to stop well-to-do parents from splurging on private schools and tutors, as they seek to give their children a leg up on the competition.

* * *

Confucianism has traditionally been associated with overzealous parenting — as aptly illustrated by Amy Chua in her controversial book, *Battle Hymn of the Tiger Mother* — and no doubt there is an element of truth to it. As Chua observes, "In China today, even little kids often study and drill from 7:00 A.M. to 10:00 P.M., grades are publicly posted, and no one's ever heard of a sleepover".[14] The situation is similar in all other Confucian societies, namely Japan, Korea, Taiwan, Vietnam, and Singapore, where millions of children attend cram schools and tutoring sessions every evening. East Asian education may be highly effective at imparting a defined set of knowledge — according to the OECD report *Education at a Glance 2011*, four out of the top five performers were Confucian societies — but it has also been criticized for over-reliance on rote memorization, top-down instructional style, and university entrance exams which strain students and parents alike.[15]

The growing link between money and education is a problem in China, just as it is in America. We have mentioned how school districts are assigned by zip codes in America; a similar problem exists in China, where its quota system is based on residency. According to one estimate, a student from Anhui province faces a one in 7,826 chances of getting into Beijing University, whereas the odds for a Beijing student are one in 190.[16] Residents in richer cities and provinces enjoy educational advantage as well, as the best schools tend to be concentrated in their localities. Meanwhile, the affluent are doing what they can to stay ahead, by sending their children to expensive international schools. When Harrow, the prestigious secondary school in England, announced it planned to open a new campus in Hong Kong, it saw a flood of applications which drove up the price of "school bond" (capital certificates giving priority for admission) to HK$3 million, or roughly US$400,000.[17] Even then, the waiting lists are as long as three years. Kellett School, another top international school in Hong Kong, advises on its website that an applicant should purchase either its "Foundation Debenture (current price HK$10 million, refundable)" or "Foundation Certificate (current price HK$5 million, non-refundable)." Imagine forking over this kind of money just to join the waitlist! One result is that even wealthy investment banks have difficulty relocating employees from Europe to Hong Kong.[18] Ouch.

In this chapter, we will not tackle the problem of money and education directly. Instead, we will leverage the Confucian theory of learning to redefine the purpose and nature of education. In doing so, we hope to convince our readers of two points: first, someone who fails to gain entry to an elite university does not have to feel like a failure for the rest of his life, because one can be as successful and happy as anybody without a gold-plated degree — or an exceptionally high IQ, for that matter. This is the truly radical egalitarianism of Confucianism, which maintains that anybody can achieve sagehood, given one's choices and efforts. Second, education should be social, emotional, and physical as much as conceptual. In the current environment, too many graduates of so-called top universities end up being one-dimensional individuals, capable of solving complex equations but lacking the moral capacity to handle life's most important problems. Combined, these two points will lead us to see that there are more important things to life than getting a degree — and help alleviate the anxiety associated with hyper-competition in education.

Redefining the Purpose of Education

Traditionally, education for most people took place either at home (for general skills such as farming, sewing, and animal husbandry) or at workshops (for specialized crafts such as baking, tailoring, and metalworking). The notion that a state has to provide free education for all would have seemed absurd in a pre-industrial society. So why did states get involved in the business of education? The primary motivation was economic. Mass education was born in the West as a response to the industrial revolution. As workshops gave way to factories, nations realized they needed a stable supply of workers with basic reading, writing, and arithmetic competencies. Hence mandatory primary education was born in the late 19th century, followed by universal secondary education in the mid-20th century. Some European nations now provide free college education as well.

Even today, the rationale for education is usually couched in economic terms. See, for example, how Friedman and Mandelbaum describe the educational challenge of America in the 21st century:

> Because of the merger of globalization and the IT revolution, raising math, science, reading, and creativity levels in American schools is the key determinant of economic growth… That is why it is no accident that President Obama has declared that "the country that out-educates us today will out-compete us tomorrow."[19]

While we accept that education is one of the key determinants of economic success in the modern world, we feel uncomfortable framing the goal of education in this manner. For one thing, the link between education and economic growth is not as straightforward as some proclaim, even in the so-called knowledge economy. As Ha-Joon Chang points out, "There is remarkably little evidence showing that more education leads to greater national prosperity".[20] For instance, back in 1960, Taiwan had literacy rate of only 54% while the corresponding figure for the Philippines was 72%. Apparently the education gap did not matter, as Taiwan went on to record one of the fastest growth rates in the world; its GDP per capita is now roughly 10 times that of the Philippines. Another example given by Chang is that of Switzerland, which has one of the lowest rates of university enrolment among rich countries (47%) but does much better economically than well-educated peers such as Greece (91%). In a much-cited study titled "Where has all the education gone?" Lant Prichett of Harvard University convincingly shows that the supposed link between education and economic growth is tenuous at best.[21]

Besides, acquisition of skills is merely one part of succeeding in the real world. To be sure, proficiency in math, reading, and science, as well as creativity and critical thinking, all matter, but what about character and discipline? Friedman and Mandelbaum argue that modern employers look for workers "who can think critically, who can tackle nonroutine complex tasks, and who can work collaboratively with teams located in their office or globally" — and these are entry-level requirements which must be met "just to get a job interview".[22] The implication, according to Friedman and Mandelbaum, is that everyone must become "creative creators" or "creative servers" — or perish. Defined this way, the challenge for educators today appears impossibly daunting. But then, amidst all the hyperbole about the hyper-connected world, we cannot help wondering whether the truth is not more mundane. The world may have changed, but not by that much. If we were to employ somebody today, we would still prioritize good-old trustworthiness and work ethic over any fancy analytical or communication skills.

In general, it can be argued that modern education has tended to over-emphasize acquisition of knowledge and skills at the expense of character-building. The former is mainly conceptual, while the latter is social, emotional, and physical. Focusing on national competitiveness as the goal of education would almost surely neglect the latter, to the detriment of the long-term health of a society. Our contention is that modern education must rediscover the importance of cultivating character, placing it among its paramount goals — and this is where Confucianism comes in.

The Moral Animal

Our view of human nature necessarily shapes our approach to education. To make a rather sweeping generalization, the West has tended to see human nature in a negative light. Plato held that human emotion was something fickle and unreliable, an inferior function to be controlled by transcendental "reason." Christianity taught that all men were born sinners and salvation lay in renouncing earthly desires. Freud argued that infantile sexual pleasures formed the basis of our character, suggesting that "civilization" was only made possible by "sublimating" our libido. Expressions may vary, but the underlying message remains the same: human nature is unruly and it is only by suppressing it that we can lead civilized lives. In this context, the role of education would be to smother our natural instincts in order to enforce socially desirable behavior. Although the reality of Western education was not nearly as bad, an expression of this view was given by Plato in *The Republic*, in the form of a totalitarian education philosophy which separates children from their parents at birth, bans sentimental music and poetry, and builds austere discipline through gymnastics.

In contrast, Confucius held a benign view of human nature. What his view meant in practice was that he affirmed the validity of our natural emotions and desires, including all of our delights, angers, sorrows, and pleasures, seeing them as a reliable basis for our value judgments. Mencius took this line of thinking even further, suggesting that our innate moral impulse is at least as strong as our desire for sex and food.[23] In fact, it can even override the survival instinct itself:

> If a man desires nothing more than to live, then there won't be anything he would not do to preserve his life. If a man hates nothing more than to die, then there won't be anything he would not do to avoid death. However, there are cases when men by a certain course may preserve life, and they do not employ it; when by certain things they may avoid danger, and they will not do them. Therefore, [we may surmise that] men like some things more than to live, and dislike some things more than to die. Such sentiments are not restricted only to the wise. All men have such feelings, but the wise take care not to lose them.[24]

This view is obviously quite different from those of the aforementioned Western thinkers. We can define human nature in terms of original sin (the Christian view), monetary desire (the economists' view), or sexual impulse (the Freudian view), but is that all there is to human nature? Surely not. Ask any economist why some people willingly give up their lives in a battle: they will roll their eyes, because no economic theory has ever explained an act of self-sacrifice. The simple truth is that all of us are driven as much by our sense of right and wrong as by any selfish desire. To borrow Robert Wright's book title, we are all moral animals. (We are using the expression with irony, because Wright's argument in *The Moral Animal* is that all our higher instincts have been designed by selfish genes — and are thus questionable. Our rebuttal would be that it doesn't matter where our selfless instincts have come from, as long as they are selfless.) Rather than define human nature as greedy and sinful, why not acknowledge that humans are also noble beings capable of altruistic acts? The role of philosophy should be to encourage and nurture the better angels of our nature, not to unearth and endorse our darker motives.

Of course, the fact that we have innate moral nature does not necessarily mean we act honorably most of the time. Inner decency is like a seed which needs to be carefully tended to, which might otherwise wither away. See how Mencius describes the process:

> The Niu mountain was once full of beautiful trees. Being situated, however, in the borders of a big city, they were hewn down with large and small axes. How could the forest retain its beauty? Still, through the activity of the vegetative life day and night, and the nourishing influence of the rain and dew, they were not without buds and sprouts springing forth, but then came the cattle and goats which grazed upon them. That is why the mountain now appears bare and stripped. People now see it, and they think it was never finely wooded, but is this the true nature of the mountain? And so also of what properly belongs to man. Shall it be said that the mind of any man was without benevolence and righteousness? The way in which a man loses his proper goodness of mind is like the way in which the trees are denuded by large and small axes. Hewn down day after day, how can the mind retain its beauty?[25]

Here Mencius is saying that even if human nature prefers beauty, the corrupting influence of civilization can easily lay waste to its goodness. The role of education, then, is to remind us of our proper nature and to bring our inner saint to the fore. This approach transcends the simplistic dichotomy of nature versus nurture. The former says that upbringing does not really matter because DNA determines everything including one's intelligence and emotional disposition (so-called genetic determinism); the latter claims that environmental factors alone can account for our behavioral traits, because one's mind is a "blank slate" (*tabula rasa*) at birth. Both are extreme views, as we obviously cannot ignore one or the other. Nurture does matter, but it becomes effective only when it takes nature into account. The real key is to work *with* nature rather than against it, so that a child may realize his kindly nature and become the good person he is perfectly capable of becoming. As the Confucian classic *Record on the Subject of Education* proclaims, "To properly realize what Heaven has given us, rather than suppress or damage it, is called good studies".[26] Dewey would have heartily agreed. According to him, the right method of education is "to direct growth through putting [natural] powers to the best possible use".[27] Assisting the spontaneous growth, rather than stunting and perverting it, is the ideal.

Beyond Freedom and Discipline

Broadly speaking, current educational philosophies can be classified into two camps: the "essentialists" or traditionalists on one hand, and the "progressives" or liberals on the other. The former emphasize rigid adherence to core curriculum and the disciplinary role of teachers, while the latter uphold flexible, task-based learning combined with the collaborative role of teachers. So which approach is correct — imposing discipline or allowing freedom?

Probably neither. A more nuanced view is that of Alfred North Whitehead, who has expounded the notion of "the rhythmic claims of freedom and discipline".[28] Whitehead's view is that adolescence must be "the period of romance." Childhood is filled with wonders, and cramming systemic knowledge at this stage can be counterproductive. Children by nature have insatiable curiosity, and the goal at this stage should be to animate their interests. Think of the Montessori system, which allows children to independently "discover" new concepts. It is then followed by "the period of precision," as students in secondary schools master the basics of language, mathematics, and science in a disciplined fashion. Here rote-learning and repetitive practices are not only permissible but essential. The aim is not to dull young minds with barren facts, but to utilize a student's natural craving for expansion to impart a carefully defined set of relevant facts, concepts, and techniques. The grip should be relaxed again once the students reach the university level, in what Whitehead calls "the period of generalization." Instead of bending over his desk, a college student should "stand up and look around" so that he may imaginatively consider general theories on the basis of specific facts.[29]

This is only a rough guideline. In practice, there are many sub-cycles at each stage of growth. For example, as a child begins the secondary level, he may already be building precision in his language but only entering a period of romance in science. Even after the child grows up, fascination with a new subject can easily initiate another romance, to be followed by concentrated study (the period of precision) and imaginative mastery (the period of generalization).

We have covered Whitehead's theory of education in some detail, because we want to show that freedom versus discipline is a false dichotomy, just like nature versus nurture. Again, education should strengthen and harness the natural impetus of a student, not smother it. The key here is to spike the student's natural desire for learning — which is the whole point of having the stage of romance run its course first — so that he will be self-motivated to put up with hard work later on. Ideally, motivation should come from within, because then the only discipline that is required is *self-discipline*. As Whitehead masterfully formulates it, "I hold that the only discipline, important for its own sake, is self-discipline, and that this can only be acquired by a wise use of freedom".[30] The goal is not to build a robot which can only do what it has been told, but to develop an autonomous human being who continues to enjoy exploring, training, and imagining on his own, long after he enters society. Incidentally, this is also the best way to ensure that our young are able to adapt to and prosper in fast-changing modern economy.

Confucian Theory of Education

The proper aim of education is to cultivate autonomy and self-discipline, which is just another way of saying that it is all about building character. This may sound like stating the obvious, but as we have seen, both traditional and liberal approaches come up short in this regard. Traditionalists seek to impose discipline from without, until the student loses whatever innate curiosity and motivation he might have once had: think of the East Asian education today, which has long been criticized not only for placing enormous strain on students, but also for killing initiative and hobbling creativity. The liberalist approach, on the other hand, tends to over-indulge children to the point of neglect, and it is rightly blamed for the decline in academic standards. A prime example is the "liberal" American educational system, which patently fails to inject basic knowledge into many of its students at the secondary level.

So how exactly do we go about reinforcing our good tendencies and building a lifelong habit of self-cultivation? We have seen one part of the answer, namely that educators must leverage, rather than run roughshod over, the natural sense of wonder and romance of a child. This insight is most useful for maximizing the effectiveness of conceptual education, but there are also emotional, physical, and social dimensions to education which we must consider. Let us now delve into the Confucian theory of education, which truly has much to say about this matter. While the Confucian literature on this subject is vast and varied, here we will focus on four rather unique features of its teachings which we feel we should be stressing today: (1) love of learning; (2) emotion over reason; (3) the importance of *kung-fu*; and (4) restoring family education.

1. Love of learning

We begin with Confucius's view of learning (rather than teaching) because ultimately education is about *self-enlightenment*. Perhaps more than any other quality, lifelong learning was the hallmark of a Confucian gentleman. Confucius was not born with any wealth, status, or even exceptional intelligence (at least not in the modest way he describes himself). All he had was his unparalleled desire to study, which enabled him to become the patron saint of Eastern civilization. As Confucius proudly proclaims:

> Even in a village with ten families, there should be someone as loyal and trustworthy as I am. But you would not find anybody who loves to learn as much as I do.[31]

Loyalty and trustworthiness are not easy qualities to acquire, but they alone do not complete a human being. Although a villager may be sincere in his intent, he might also be obstinate and narrow-minded, unable to accept conflicting viewpoints or changes to his old ways — that is, unless he is willing to break out of his shell and learn new things. For Confucius, the love of learning signified a willingness to keep an open mind and constantly enlarge his horizon of understanding. It also meant being humble about what he already knew, as illustrated by the following episode in the *Analects*:

> Confucius entered the Grand Temple [for the first time]. Every step of the way, he would ask a question. Someone said, "Who says that the guy from Tsau province [i.e. Confucius] knows manners! He enters the Grand Temple and has to ask about everything." Confucius heard the remark and answered, "That I ask is manners".[32]

The irony here is that Confucius was widely considered the authority on the rules of propriety. He was appointed minister of justice in the state of Lu, partly because of his acknowledged expertise on ancient texts and rites. Nevertheless, when attending a ceremony at the Grand Temple for the first time (commoners were not allowed to enter), he enquires about every small detail to the point of being embarrassing. That is why someone cannot help sneering, "Who says this country bumpkin is an expert on ceremonies!" Confucius retorts that the act of asking is itself the highest form of manners, as it shows respect for others, consideration of situational factors, and tolerance for different ways of thinking.

As we contemplate his curt but profound reply, we cannot help being amazed by the unassuming, unorthodox stance of our beloved master. Compare his humility and open-mindedness to the dogmatic self-righteousness of religious teachers elsewhere — from Saint Paul to Justin Martyr to Augustinus of Hippo to Martin Luther — who had no hesitation in denouncing all non-believers as sons of darkness or agents of Satan. We close this discussion with another touching remark by Confucius, one which reinforces our point that love of learning is really about the ability to break out of one's shell and embrace differences — and to do so ceaselessly throughout life:

> Even when I travel with only two people, there should be a teacher for me in the group. I choose the good one and follow his fine qualities, while using the bad one to identify what to correct about myself.[33]

2. Emotion over reason

As noted previously, the original meaning of *ren* was "an ability to feel." Confucius placed a high value on emotional responses when it came to forming value judgments. This is difficult for Western readers to grasp, because Western philosophers from Plato onward have maintained the superiority of reason over emotion. Reason in the Western tradition primarily referred to the ability to calculate. The term "rational" comes from the Latin word *ratio*, which means computation. Legend has it that the door of Plato's Academy was engraved with these words: "Let no one ignorant of geometry enter." For Plato, geometry represented the path to unchanging, ultimate truth, whereas emotion was regarded as something unreliable, an inferior function to be subdued by reason. Confucius held an opposite view. The ability to calculate "$1 + 1 = 2$" was deemed a rather basic function. What Confucius sought to cultivate instead was sophistication of our sensibility.

It is only with the advance of cognitive psychology in the 20th century that the West has come to accept (slowly and grudgingly) the primacy of emotion in our internal decision-making. Our emotional response is a highly complex phenomenon which defies easy explanation in terms of cause and effect. Whereas reason only deals with the conscious part of our brain, our emotional response (gut feeling, intuition) encompasses the *totality* of our senses, experiences, and subconscious reasoning. That is why Confucius regarded it as a higher form of judgment than reason. And our sensibility is not static: it evolves through experience, and it can also be refined through education.

Human beings are creatures of emotion. We like to pretend otherwise, but the greater part of our daily lives is dominated by flows of emotion. At work, a thoughtless email or phone call from a co-worker can ruin your day. A recent study in the UK found that couples at home argue on average 2,455 times a year, or seven times a day, mostly over trivial things such as not closing cupboard doors or forgetting to take things when they go upstairs.[34] Even in politics and business, emotion accounts for a far larger portion of our judgment than we often realize. Seen this way, emotion may indeed seem like something negative, a lurking beast which we must control by reason (Plato's view) or renounce altogether (the Buddhist view).

Confucius also sought to "master" emotion, but in a very different way. Rather than suppress emotion, he sought to nurture and harness it. He had a fundamentally positive view of human nature, which in practice meant affirming the validity of our natural emotions and desires. Having appropriate emotion is infinitely more enjoyable than smothering it or having no feeling at all. As David Brooks observes in *The Social Animal*, "The key to a well-lived life is to have trained the emotions to send the right signals and to be sensitive to their subtle calls".[35] An important aim of education, then, is to cultivate an emotionally sensitive individual, who can manage his feelings of delight, anger, sorrow, and pleasure in a balanced manner, with a view to controlling excesses (too much pleasure can be just as harmful to our health as too much sorrow) and maintaining social harmony (this is not necessarily being conformist but being socially attuned and cooperative).

Education is as much about cultivating emotional maturity as it is about developing our mental capabilities. In fact, having a gentle and sympathetic disposition is the very definition of what it means to be civilized as a human being. As things stand today, we have too many highly trained minds who become inconsiderate snobs with no sense of what is proper, and the most ambitious among them end up as con-artists in Wall Street or spin-masters in Washington. Unless we recognize that morality is primarily a matter of having the right emotional disposition rather than an ability to make rational (read: cold and calculating) judgments, we may never be able to restore humaneness and benevolence to our society. This is why educators must not only convey knowledge but also nurture our sensibility (*ren*).

3. Importance of *kung-fu*

Having the right emotional disposition is only the beginning. The difficult part is in keeping up good behavior until it becomes a habit, or even a second nature; this is what is meant by building character. Let us illustrate this point by quoting a passage from the Bible:

> You have heard that it was said, "You shall not commit adultery." But I say to you that everyone who looks at a woman lustfully has already committed adultery with her in his heart. (Matthew 5:27–28)

With all due respect to our beloved Jesus, this is pure nonsense. Having a momentary thought cannot be the same as having repetitive thoughts or actually acting upon it. The problem with Jesus's reasoning here is that it fails to take into account the element of *time*. Every virtue or vice is not a virtue or vice until some time has elapsed. If someone quits smoking today, it does not mean that he is a non-smoker. If he can continue for at least three months — well, then we might as well acknowledge that he has indeed stopped smoking. It means that his *body* no longer needs nicotine as badly as it used to.

Deciding to quit smoking, or having a lustful thought, is an act of mind. But one's body is a system of inertia carrying ingrained habits. To really quit smoking, or to be able to see a woman in a non-lustful way, we have to train our bodies that way. The bodily discipline thus built is what Confucians called *kung-fu*. Although in the West the term primarily refers to Chinese martial arts, it originally denoted excellence in any discipline, somewhat similar to Aristotle's concept of virtue (*arete*). An accomplished cook or carpenter possesses as much *kung-fu* as any *Tai Chi* master; the common denominator is that both take years of physical training. As Wang Bi observed in his annotation of *Tao Te Ching*, "Virtue means accumulation",[36] and the process of accumulating good habits takes time.

The implication here is that we should guide our children in building the right habits from early on. We need to focus less on the rote memorization of facts (which they will forget anyway) and more on instilling good physical habits (which will last a lifetime). Some of the fundamentals may include: having good manners, cleaning up after oneself, not lying, being punctual, keeping the right posture, and sitting at one's desk for a long stretch, day after day. The last is what the Germans call *sitzfleisch* — literally, the ability to sit, or, as a satirical writer Tim Kreider puts it, "to spend serious time at something, devote your sustained attention to a single subject for four, six or eight hours, and resist the impulse to get up and take a break or check e-mail when you get fidgety or bored".[37] Without exaggeration, we believe it is the single most important discipline (*kung-fu*) a child can acquire if he is to achieve anything noteworthy with his life.

4. Restoring family education

In Eastern folklore, Mencius is known better for what his mother did to teach him than for any of his actual teachings. Mencius's father passed away when he was only three years old, so his education was completely left to his mother. There is a famous Chinese expression, "Mencius's mother, three moves," meaning that his mother moved three times in order to find a suitable environment for her son's upbringing. This legend is often cited by overzealous Asian parents to justify overinvestment in education, and in that sense, Mencius's mother may be considered the iconic Tiger Mother. But that is not why we introduce her example here.

There are two messages we want to convey with regard to family education: first, parents should be more involved in their children's upbringing. The rise of mass education in the 20th century has led too many parents to abdicate their responsibility and outsource the education of their children to the state — and they blame school teachers when things go wrong! Some parents may argue that leaving children alone is a more liberal approach which respects their natural growth and autonomy. But it does not cultivate character. Our good values, habits, and tastes do not pass down automatically through genes. They are communicated through myriad verbal interactions, including through parental demands, encouragements, and disapprovals. That is why it matters that parents spend as much time as possible doing things together with their children. Barring those joint activities, children would have great difficulty developing fully as social beings.

Which brings us to our second point: parents must be continually conscious of what examples their actions are setting for their children. Let us introduce a prosaic yet touching episode from *The Outer Commentary to the Book of Songs by Master Han*: When Mencius was a boy, he saw a neighbor slaughter a pig. He asked his mother, "Why are they killing the pig?" The mother casually joked, "To give it to you." Then she quickly realized her mistake and went to her neighbor to actually buy some meat — normally she was too poor to do so — because she did not want to teach lying to her son.

For a more modern example, here is how Zac Bissonnette, the author of *How to Be Richer, Smarter, and Better-Looking Than Your Parents*, advises parents on inculcating the right financial values, which really makes us think twice about flaunting our wealth:

> Do I think parents who drive luxury cars set a bad image for kids? ...It sets the idea that this stuff is important in life. They're learning that this stuff can make you happier, and you can rely on mass-produced goods for some sort of fulfillment. And you can't.[38]

Actions by parents exercise educative and formative influences, often unconsciously and without any set purpose, because children instinctively emulate their ideas, beliefs, and emotional attitudes. Children do not grow up fantasizing about sex with their parents, as Freud claimed. Instead, their super-egos are formed each and every time parents make value judgments in front of them. This means that parents had better practice what they preach — an extremely demanding requirement, if one stops and thinks about it. There is no other way, though, as we cannot really fool our children. Simply put, our actions speak louder than words. Bettering our children begins with bettering ourselves.

Talent, Discipline, and Success

Let us now return to the question of whether having a degree from an elite university, or an exceptionally high IQ, matters to our long-term success and happiness. Here is how Hsun Tzu thought of the issue of innate talent:

> The finest horse, called the Thousand-League Horse, can run one thousand leagues a day. But even the slowest horse can cover the same distance in ten days.[39]

What Hsun Tzu means is that setting the right goal and being persistent in pursuing it matters as much as being gifted. The more modern expression of this view was given by Malcolm Gladwell in *Outliers*. In the book, Gladwell proposes what he calls the "10,000-hour rule," which states that truly excelling in any given field takes roughly 10,000 hours of practice. As examples, he cites Mozart, the Beatles, Bill Joy, and Bill Gates, and he convincingly demonstrates that all of them have, "through a combination of ability, opportunity, and utterly arbitrary advantage," managed to accumulate over 10,000 hours of focused training as young adults, which he calls "a critical minimum level of practice".[40] Even Mozart, who is often thought of as a child prodigy, did not compose any of his masterpieces until the age of 21, when he had already been writing concertos for 10 years.[41]

The takeaway here is that a strong work ethic matters at least as much as talent in determining one's prospects. To be sure, some people find it easier to put up with the slog than others, and we may say they are more "talented" in that sense. Spending eight hours a day, seven days a week, in front of a computer terminal was probably not all that painful for the young Bill Gates, whereas it could be a tough grind for others. But the important point is that there is no avoiding clocking the hours. If you do clock the hours — through talent, luck, or plain dumb willpower — then you, too, may achieve remarkable things. It all leads us back to the importance of building the right habits.

* * *

According to Confucius, doing something extraordinary is relatively easy, since it is a one-off event. The hard thing is to keep up unexciting but healthy routines in our ordinary daily lives. As Zisi quotes him in the *Doctrine of the Mean*:

> One can pacify the world, turn down fame and fortune, and step upon the sharpest blade. But one cannot maintain the mean.[42]

Maintaining the mean — here it means sustaining sound habits every day — is considered the most difficult achievement, precisely because it is so agonizingly dull and boring. Persevering with one's resolution is not easy. Take running, for example. We all know that running every morning is one of the best ways to keep fit, to build stamina, and to start the day with a clear mind. So why not just do it? It is because we can find a million excuses not to run on a particular morning.

Keeping up a good habit is challenging, because one is always tempted to skip just one day. There is always tomorrow to start over again, right? Confucius had a simple antidote to this temptation: find one good habit, start immediately, and stick with it for three months.[43] As anyone who has committed to a New Year's resolution can testify, persevering with a good habit for three months is quite a challenge. The challenge is worthwhile, though, because if you can hold onto a habit for three months, you can usually continue it for life. Repeat this formula for one small habit after another, and you might well transform yourself into a completely different person — a kind of revolution from within — and you can plausibly excel in almost anything you set your mind to.

Until now we have not really touched upon our personal stories in this book, but allow us to introduce one here: Young-oak was the

youngest child in his family. All of his older brothers graduated from
Kyunggi, the most prestigious secondary school in Korea at the time.
Young-oak did not get in, and it was a source of an inferiority complex for him. He lived with his oldest brother when he was young. All
four sons of the brother had also attended Kyunggi, and as such, even
some of his nephews did not show much respect to him. Then, one
day, he had an epiphany: "The truly important thing in life is to gain
the respect of the people closest to me — my mother, brother, brother's wife, and nephews — not necessarily by getting the best degree,
but by conducting myself in the most exemplary manner." He started
his day by cleaning up after himself. Every morning, he would fold
the sheets and wipe the room dustless, followed by a morning run.
Then he would spend long hours at his desk studying (recall what we
said about *sitzfleisch*) until his body ached. At night, he would make
an entry in his diary, taking stock of what he had achieved that day.
Gradually, the way his family members looked at him changed,
evolving from curiosity and shock to wonderment and awe.

Taken individually, none of these is an extraordinary habit, but
they are the routines which Young-oak has continued for four decades now, day after day — even as he started a family, earned a
Harvard PhD, became a tenured professor, began lecturing on
national TV, and emerged as the leading intellectual in Korea. The
diary he started keeping while in college continues to this date. He is
far from perfect, but at least he can match any yogi or ascetic monk
in his bodily discipline (*kung-fu*). To be sure, such discipline and
hard work by themselves do not guarantee worldly success, but we
do believe they represent probably the surest way to find lasting happiness and fulfilment in life. So what about that all-important
degree?

> The Master said, "In archery we have something like the way of the gentle-
> man. When the archer misses the centre of the target, he turns around and
> seeks the cause of his failure in himself."[44]

Here Confucius compares the way of the gentleman to archery;
the analogy can be applied to education as well. Just as the goal post
in soccer is not the "goal" of soccer, the target cannot be the "goal"
of archery. The target is just there as a means to guide our

movements. The real art of archery lies in assuming the correct stance, loading the arrow and raising the bow the right way, and keeping one's body still while aiming and releasing. That is why the archer "seeks the cause of his failure in himself" when the target is missed.

Likewise, earning admission to an elite university cannot be the goal of education. It is just an "end-in-view" (to use Dewey's expression) which is there to guide our actions, but not the actual end. Suppose a soccer player who has practiced shooting for years somehow misses his target by inches. Does that mean he is not a good soccer player? Of course not. Suppose a student patiently studies for years to apply to Harvard University, but for whatever reason the admissions committee turns him down (Harvard rejects hundreds of high-school valedictorians and students with perfect SAT scores each year). Does that mean he is not a good student? No! Although some parents may fret that the result is all that matters, we must not be fooled into thinking that the goal of education is some kind of degree or qualification, or anything which is external to ourselves. What really matters is whether the student has attained a level of self-discipline — ideally, the habit of ceaselessly cultivating himself and learning on his own — which is not only intrinsically rewarding, but will also allow him to prosper and succeed in the long voyage of life.

Moral Leadership

In his moving last lecture at Carnegie Mellon, Randy Pausch describes the method of indirect learning which he calls the "head fake." For example, most parents do not enrol their children in a football program to teach football techniques *per se*, the three-point stance and chop block, and all that. The true purpose is to instil the values of teamwork, sportsmanship, and perseverance. At the end of his lecture, Pausch reveals that the whole lecture has in fact been a "head fake." Although the lecture was titled "Really Achieving Your Childhood Dreams," the lecture was not really about how to achieve one's dreams. Rather, it was about how to live one's life the right way.[45] The Confucian method of education is similarly indirect. Although it necessarily starts with some kind of curriculum — the original Six Arts of Confucianism were comprised of rites, music, archery, charioteering, calligraphy, and mathematics — the real goal is not to inject a defined set of knowledge or to impose certain kinds of behavior, but rather to instil the lifelong habit of self-cultivation, so that one may eventually realize the ideal of sagehood.

We have mentioned the term "sagehood" several times in this book, but we never explained what it is. What exactly is a "sage"? See how Hsun Tzu defines the concept:

> A sage is someone who practices the highest degree of morality; a king is someone who practices the highest degree of institutional management. Having both, one could serve as the penultimate example for the world. This is why someone who has set his mind upon learning would take the ancient sage king as a role model, and take his laws as an exemplary institution... and then ultimately seek to emulate the very personality of the sage king himself.[46]

Here the sage is defined as someone who personifies the highest degree of virtue, thereby serving as an inspirational example for people. In other words, the sage is a guardian of moral values who "teaches" by leading his life the right way, so that his virtues may permeate the rest of society. The king, on the other hand, is a ruler who manages the institution of government. The ideal king is defined as someone who combines the pragmatic expertise of a king with the virtue of a sage, whom Hsun Tzu calls the "sage king," in a not-so-distant parallel to Plato's conception of the "philosopher king." Confucius held that such kings had actually existed in ancient times — Yao and Shun of the legendary Xia dynasty being the two paramount examples — and Hsun Tzu suggests that a Confucian gentleman emulate their ways.

In modern times, we might as well substitute the expression "sage king" with "moral leader." A moral leader is an administrator *and* teacher who provides ethical guidance to his society, not just by saying the right things, but by setting the right example. We want our readers to dwell on that last sentence for a moment: is this not the very definition of moral leadership — in fact, what leadership should be all about? We stated earlier that, more than anything else, Confucianism is a leadership development philosophy. Specifically, the kind of leadership it sought to develop was moral leadership, which could transform a society by awakening the innate goodness in its members.

The ultimate goal of self-cultivation, then, is nothing short of changing the world. The *Great Learning*, one of the Four Books of Confucianism (along with the *Analects*, *Mencius*, and the *Doctrine of the Mean*), describes the process as follows:

> The ancients, who wished to illustrate illustrious virtue throughout the world, first ordered well their own states. Wishing to order well their states, they first regulated their families. Wishing to regulate their families, they first cultivated their persons... Their persons being cultivated, their families were regulated. Their families being regulated, their states were rightly governed. Their states being rightly governed, the entire world was at peace.[47]

Here the author declares that realizing world peace starts with self-cultivation; bettering the world begins by bettering ourselves. The corollary is that sagehood is not just about personal ethics. It necessarily involves social realization, because human beings are social by nature. Fulfilling family and social obligations lies at the centre of what it means to lead a meaningful and satisfactory life. One achieves sagehood not by meditating alone on a mountaintop, but by constantly interacting with his family, friends, co-workers, and other members of his community, with a view to shaping his society for the better. As Stephen Angle, who teaches philosophy at Wesleyan University, observes, "[O]n any traditional Confucian's view... striving for personal betterment and social betterment are really one and the same process".[48] Just to be clear, personal betterment here does not simply mean the acquisition of new knowledge; it also means cultivating moral character by building one's emotional, physical, and social capabilities.

* * *

We have seen in the preceding chapters that institutional reforms alone cannot solve our problems in government and business. As things currently stand, lawmakers have to constantly develop increasingly complex regulations because our politicians and businessmen are getting ever better at dodging the existing ones. Take the financial services industry, for example: remember the Dodd–Frank Wall Street Reform and Consumer Protection Act, which ran on for 2,300 pages? Unfortunately, judging from the recent scandals involving brokerage frauds (MF Global), rate-rigging (Barclays), and money laundering (HSBC), the bill is a toothless tiger which has conspicuously failed to inject discipline into our financial services industry. So what is to be done? Shall we introduce even greater government oversight and compliance requirements, which will probably do nothing to restore morality to our banking system, but provide a boon to our lawyers, accountants, and tax advisors? No, what we need is something else entirely: true leaders who have the moral power to transform our culture.

Chapter

5

The New China Model

What makes a great nation is its being like a low-lying downstream.

Tao Te Ching, verse 61

Rise of the "China model"

After the Berlin Wall fell in 1989, Francis Fukuyama famously declared that what we were witnessing was not just the end of the Cold War but the "end of history as such," in the sense that the socio-economic evolution of mankind had reached its peak in the triumph of Western liberal democracy. The implication was that liberal democracy, combined with "Anglo-Saxon" capitalism, was the ultimate form of social organization toward which all nations would sooner or later converge.

How times have changed. In a striking act of *mea culpa* — one journalist jokingly called it "the end of the end of history" — Fukuyama recently wrote in the *Financial Times* that the American model "has little to teach China".[1] Whatever moral high ground America may once have had, America "managed to fritter away... in a remarkably short order" due to "militarised and unilateral" foreign policy, as evidenced in the invasion of Iraq, and more recently, the US-led global financial crisis. In the meantime, the Chinese are on a roll, thanks to its non-democratic but efficient government. According to Fukuyama,

> The most important strength of the Chinese political system is its ability to make large, complex decisions quickly, and to make them relatively well, at least in economic policy. This is most evident in the area of infrastructure, where China has put into place airports, dams, high-speed rail, water and electricity systems to feed its growing industrial base. Contrast this with [democratic] India, where every new investment is subject to blockage by trade unions, lobby groups, peasant associations and courts.

As a result, the Chinese are growing ever more confident that China has little to learn from America about its political or economic system. Perhaps their model of party dictatorship, combined with state-directed capitalism, is a viable alternative to Western liberal democracy after all. Many Western observers predicted that as its citizens grew wealthier, China would undergo democratic transition, just as South Korea and Taiwan did during the 1980s. For now, there is little hope of that happening. Why would the Chinese bother? The US just emerged from its own version of the Lost Decade, during which its economy kept growing but tumbled badly in-between, not once but twice (the burst of the dot-com bubble and the burst of the housing bubble). Paul Krugman dubbed the decade "Big Zero": zero job creation, zero growth in median household income, and zero gains in housing price or stock price, between December 1999 and December 2009.[2] During the same decade, China's GDP almost *quadrupled* (it quintupled in dollar terms, from around one trillion dollars a decade ago to almost five trillion in 2009, because of appreciation in the value of the *yuan*).[3] To put it another way: in 2000 America's GDP was about eight times as big as China's; now it is only twice as big. *The Economist* predicts that China will overtake the US to become the world's largest economy by 2018.[4]

The axis of power clearly seems to be shifting, from Western Europe in the 19th century to America in the 20th century to China in the 21st century. Little wonder, then, that the Chinese are growing a bit boastful. In January 2009, the Chinese government unveiled a new project called "overseas propaganda" with a view to

promoting the "China model." There was a slight problem, though:
it was unclear from official statements what they meant by the
"China model." The government newspaper *Xinhua* at the time
railed against the failures of free-market fundamentalism in the
West, and then said something about the Chinese way of doing
things under President Hu Jintao's "scientific theory of development".[5] Just as the Singaporeans had a tough time defining "Asian
values" during the 1990s, the proponents of the China model
today disagree over what the term really encompasses. As Fukuyama
wryly observes,

> But what is the Chinese model? Many observers casually put it in an "au-
> thoritarian capitalist" box, along with Russia, Iran and Singapore. But
> China's model is *sui generis*; its specific mode of governance is difficult to
> describe, much less emulate... the quality of Chinese government is higher
> than in Russia, Iran, or the other authoritarian regimes with which it is
> often lumped.

So what exactly is the China model? Well, we can tell you easily.
The bottom line is that the Chinese Communist Party rules supreme
in China. Its influence permeates almost every aspect of society. The
Chinese Communist Party is unlike the Democratic Party or the
Republican Party. The Democrats and the Republicans are political
parties which were formed to compete for power *under* the democratic state. The Chinese Communist Party, on the other hand, is an
organization which reigns *over* the state.

To outsiders, it may appear that China has all the elements of a
modern state, such as an executive government, a parliament, and a
court system. The peculiarity of China, however, is that in most cases
there are parallel party organizations which have similar functions
and oversee their government counterparts. Xi Jinping, the party secretary, ranks above Li Keqiang, the premier. The Politburo (party
leadership) presides over the State Council (the cabinet). The health
minister defers to internal party bodies governing health matters.
And so on.[6] A good illustration of this concept of the party controlling the state, according to Richard McGregor, can be found in the
car plate numbers of senior officials. The Shanghai party secretary's

number is 00001; the mayor's plate is 00002.[7] The reach of the party extends well beyond the government, to state-owned enterprises, media, universities, and even religious organizations. So, for example, the CEO of a state-owned enterprise is answerable to the party secretary of the company, who acts as if he were the chairman. The party, then, is truly a supra-national body. Even the People's Liberation Army, the world's largest military force, is organized as the military arm of the party, not of the state.

The party dictatorship may have been highly effective in the unique historical context of China, but it is hardly an inspiring "model" for other nations. Let us now elaborate how the China model should evolve in the future — not what it *is*, but what it *ought* to be — by leveraging the key insights of Confucianism which we have established.

Redefining the China model

In the preceding section, we defined the current "China model" as a party dictatorship in which the party reigns supreme over everything else, including the state apparatus, the military, and major corporations. Institutionally, this is correct. Culturally, however, things are more complicated. Martin Jacques, in his bestseller *When China Rules the World*, lists the "Confucian" characteristics of the China model, which are not unique to China but are also shared by all other Confucian societies, namely Japan, Korea, Taiwan, Vietnam, and Singapore. In the political realm, China has a paternalistic state which has no qualms about "edifying" its citizens, as the moralistic undertone of its pronouncements shows. Moral suasion, as we have seen, is central to Confucian governance.[8] In the economic realm, China is a developmental state just like the Asian Tigers; its defining characteristic is that the state does not suppress the market, but rather directs and harnesses the vibrant private sector to advance its social developmental goals. In education, Chinese parents and teachers tend to be less *laissez-faire* than their Western counterparts, establishing strict moral guidelines in terms of behavior and responsibility.[9] In short, the China model may already be more Confucian in its *modus operandi* than even some of its practitioners realize. As Jacques notes:

> ...although officially disavowed, Confucian values and ways of thinking continued to be very influential, albeit in a subterranean form, remaining in some measure the common sense of people.[10]

The remarkable endurance of Confucian influence is encouraging, but our vision of the Great Equal Society demands more. Based on discussions thus far, we believe the following are the key components of the new social agenda China should undertake:

	Cultural emphasis (primary)	Institutional measures (supplementary)
Government	Morality of the leadership	Meritocracy Freedom of the media
Economy	Profit motive as secondary	Social safety net Worker protection and product safety
Education	Lifelong self-cultivation	Better public education Fair access to higher education

Based on our arguments in the preceding chapters, the table above should be largely self-explanatory, but allow us to reiterate some general principles.

1. Government

- Moral suasion does not work without ethical leaders. When officials know that graft begins at the very top, how can they take education (or even prosecution) seriously? Eradicating corruption is not difficult. If the party leaders actually practiced what they preach, the rank-and-file would naturally fall in line. As Confucius observes, "Virtue of the leader is like the wind, and virtue of the people is like grass. Grass bends as the wind blows." Creating a virtuous society begins at the top.
- To supplement the reform, the party should consider adopting the following features of Singapore's meritocracy: (1) long-term

and flexible recruiting, which both develops talent internally and invites high-flyers from the private sector, (2) strict monitoring of performance to ensure that non-performers are weeded out, and (3) competitive salaries which not only help attract the best candidates but also make it easier for officials to resist bribes.

- The party should also reduce the role of the propaganda department and introduce genuine freedom of the media. This will help maintain public trust, while allowing Beijing to effectively monitor and respond to what is happening at the local level.

- As a side note, it is time the West recognized the legitimacy of the party dictatorship. Democracy is not an end in and of itself. It is merely a means of putting the right leaders in charge and, as Singapore demonstrates, there are other ways to achieve the same goal. Ultimately, what matters is not popular mandate *per se* but having able and selfless leaders. If the party can continue to produce such leaders, then the Chinese people will be only too happy to acknowledge its Mandate of Heaven.

2.   Economy

- A society which prizes profit-making above all else is bound to decay sooner or later. While Confucians clearly appreciated the power of markets to enrich people's lives, they also held that the profit motive (*li*) should be brought under control by the spirit of empathy (*ren*) and social justice (*yi*). Otherwise, capitalism can degenerate into a no-holds-barred competition, dehumanizing us to a point where we see one another as moneymaking tools (a means) rather than as fellow human beings (an end in itself).

- In other words, Confucianism is pro-market but only up to a point, because we cannot allow economic rationality to run roughshod over social and human considerations. This is a balanced view which transcends the simplistic dichotomy of left-wing versus right-wing, socialists versus neoliberals, etc. On one hand, it embraces freedom of commerce and low taxes as the driver of social development. On the other hand, it advocates a paternalistic state which protects the livelihood of people so that, to borrow a passage from *Mencius*, "grey-haired men will not be seen on the streets carrying heavy burdens on their backs."

- What the above means for the party is that it should break out of its addiction to GDP growth. More than anything else, it may be the relentless pursuit of wealth (*li*) at the national level which precipitated the stunning collapse in values, as it encouraged too many people to behave as if anything can be justified for the sake of making money. Instead, the party should restore the humanitarian aspirations of communism (although not its radical methods) and focus on providing economic security as well as preventing the worst excesses of capitalism. In particular, the state should bolster the social safety net and enforce labour and product safety laws.

- In the private sector, business owners should follow the example of Japan Inc. and adopt harmonious labor relations. This will be crucial if the Chinese economy is to transition from cheap manufacturing to value-added industries. After all, how can a company create great products, or deliver exceptional services, with disgruntled employees? What every great entrepreneur has in common is the spirit of social realization: pushing the frontier of technology, or providing quality products at affordable prices, for example. While a business must generate sufficient profit to cover the risks of economic activity, making money (a.k.a. maximizing shareholder value) should not be its primary goal.

3. Education

- Parents and teachers must not be fooled into thinking that the goal of education is some kind of degree or qualification; it is just an "end-in-view" which is there to guide our actions, but not the actual end. The proper aim of education is not to build a robot which can only do what it has been told, but to develop an autonomous human being who continues to enjoy exploring, training, and imagining on his own, long after he enters society. It is also the best way to ensure that the child be able to adapt to and prosper in the fast-changing modern economy.

- The ultimate goal of self-cultivation, according to Confucianism, is to become a moral leader who has the power to transform a society by awakening innate goodness in its members. Such a leader provides ethical guidance to his society, not just by saying the right things, but by setting the right example. Self-cultivation here does not simply mean the acquisition of new knowledge; it also means cultivating moral character by building one's emotional, physical, and social capabilities.

- At the macro level, the growing link between money and education is an issue in China, just as it is in the US. Improving public education should be a priority, as it is still the best way to ensure a degree of equality of opportunity as a society. Specifically, the central government should address the education gap among different provinces and provide fair access to higher education.

- Additionally, the party should consider replacing Marxist philosophy with Confucianism as a required subject. While the knowledge of the classics on its own may not produce moral individuals, it will almost certainly reintroduce concepts such as *ren*, *yi*, and *li* into daily discourse. In the long run, this will help China develop truly indigenous sociology, economics, political science, and jurisprudence. Besides, would it not be wonderful if young Chinese could cite the *Analects* with the same ease as the English-speaking elite quote Shakespeare?

What we see here is that the Great Equal Society is not a simple egalitarian, anti-capitalist agenda, but rather a comprehensive social vision, based on a creative reinterpretation of Confucianism, which seeks to change the way our government, businesses, and education system operate. We will further illustrate our vision of China's future toward the end of this chapter. Before we do so, however, let us cover two topics which matter greatly to China's future and also concern the rest of mankind: diplomacy and the environment.

On Diplomacy

According to Martin Jacques, China has traditionally not subscribed to the notion of the equality of states, because it was so huge compared with its relatively small neighbors (Korea, Mongolia, Manchuria, Tibet, Vietnam, etc.). Instead, international relations in East Asia were governed by a tributary system, which involved "neighbouring states acknowledging China's cultural superiority and its overwhelming power by rendering tribute to the Middle Kingdom... in return for benevolence and protection".[11] As the disparity between China and the rest of the region grows in both economic and military terms, it is perhaps inevitable that some features of the tributary system will reassert themselves. While this development may sound sinister to many Western readers — conjuring up an image of foreign envoys kowtowing before the emperor in Beijing — the fact is that the Chinese version of imperialism was far more benign than its Western counterpart. Not only did China lack the colonial ambition which characterized Western empires, but it also maintained a diplomatic tradition of always giving back more than it received in tributes. This tradition can trace its origin to Confucian teachings. As Confucius advises a young king in the *Doctrine of the Mean*, "Send the envoys away with liberal gifts, and welcome their coming with small contributions"[12]; it was simply seen as the proper way for a great nation to behave. Given this tradition, Yan Xuetong of Tsinghua University envisions that although China may build up hegemonic capabilities in the short term, it will increasingly become a more benevolent kind of superpower in the longer term.[13] Jacques also predicts that Chinese foreign policy in the future will differ markedly from that of the US today, and he contemplates a scenario whereby "China's ascendancy would be characterized by humane authority and would indeed represent a new kind of global leadership".[14]

Why did Confucians insist that a great nation be generous in its dealings with smaller states? To properly understand their position, we need to take a short stroll through ancient China. The Spring and Autumn period (the time of Confucius) was characterized by the breakdown of Zhou dynasty and ensuing power struggles among its fiefdoms. The Warring States period which followed (the time of Mencius) was an era defined by all-out wars of conquest and constantly changing alliances. Cunning statecraft and mutual suspicion were the norm. Tacticians traveled around the states to advise their rulers on strategy. Two of the major schools of thought in this period were called, respectively, the School of Diplomacy and the School of Military Strategies. It was against this backdrop of rampant militarism and hostile international relations that Mencius criticized the prevailing Way of the Hegemon; the alternative he put forward was called the Way of the Prince, a concept which originally appears in the *Classic of History*. Simply put, the former is about subduing opponents by sheer material strength; the latter concerns winning hearts and minds. To borrow Jacques's expression, the Way of the Prince is to accomplish one's agenda "by persuasion and force of example rather than force majeure".[15] We could also compare it to the modern concept of "soft power," which Joseph Nye of Harvard University defines as the ability to attract and co-opt rather than employing force or money.

Still, one might ask: how can soft power compete against armoured soldiers carrying swords and spears? Mencius was not being naïve when he promulgated the Way of the Prince to various rulers of his time. It is hard to imagine today, but ancient China was sparsely populated, and people were relatively free to move among states (no visa or port of entry existed back then). The key to building a powerful state therefore lay in attracting immigrants from neighboring states to increase one's own population. See, for example, the following question which King Hui of Liang poses to Mencius:

> On examining the government of the neighbouring kingdoms, I do not find that there is any prince who exerts his mind as I do. And yet the people of the neighbouring kingdoms do not decrease, nor do my people increase. How is this?[16]

Here the king makes it clear that attracting migrant population is his policy priority. Mencius's reply — which starts with the remark "Your majesty is fond of war" — is too long to introduce here, but his message is that if the king truly cared for the livelihood of his people, rather than burdening them with heavy taxes and military duties, all men under Heaven would beat a path to his door. The same principle applied to diplomacy: precisely because the Warring

States period was filled with mistrust and deceit, the king could easily become a unifying force for other rulers, only if he genuinely espoused benevolence and observed moral norms (rather than power norms) in international relations.

Back to the present: the world may have changed considerably since the Warring States period, but what constitutes a great nation remains the same. The US became a great nation primarily due to its soft power — specifically, its ability to attract talented immigrants as well as the moral authority it enjoys (at least among its allies) — rather than through its military might. It may surprise you when we say that China must open its door to immigrants, given how crowded it already is, but the truth is that almost every great nation in history has been an open society which accommodated foreigners of all stripes. A great nation also embraces smaller states into its orbit, providing stability and moral leadership. Such nature of a great nation is beautifully captured in the following verse from *Tao Te Ching*, which compares a great nation to the "downstream" of a river:

> What makes a great nation is its being like a low-lying downstream. It becomes the centre to which all the small nations under Heaven tend. [To illustrate from] the case of all females: the female always overcomes the male by her stillness. Stillness may be considered a kind of humility... A great nation only wishes to unite men together and nourish them; a small nation only wishes to be received by, and to serve, the other. Each gets what it desires, but the great nation must learn to lie low.[17]

Here the sage of Taoism advocates a kind of feminine role for a great nation, which contrasts sharply with the muscular military expansionism of the US. If China follows his profound wisdom, then it will come to represent a very different kind of global leadership which the world may well welcome and celebrate.

Ultimately, the best way to understand Mencius's theory of diplomacy is to recall his dichotomy of benevolence (*ren*) and profit (*li*). Diplomacy based purely on *li* is Machiavellian in the sense that expedient pragmatism trumps loyalty or moral considerations. The problem with this approach is that no real trust can exist among nations. As such, it is very difficult for them to cooperate on any common cause. By way of illustration, the aforementioned School of Diplomacy was also known as the School of Vertical and Horizontal Alliances. In the event, whether alliances were vertical or horizontal did not matter, as mutual suspicion among allied states quickly led to the breakdown of such alliances. This kind of diplomacy, which assumes the worst about human nature, may be suited to a zero-sum world where nations compete for finite land and resources. However, in the hyper-connected modern world where humanity has so much to gain from cooperating — and so much to lose from failing to do so — the more appropriate approach would be diplomacy based on *ren*, i.e. the Way of the Prince.

It might all sound hopelessly naïve. Our diplomats and generals are by nature a suspicious bunch who have been trained to assume the worst about one another's intentions. All the same, it is time they learned to give one another the benefit of doubt — or, even better, to be unselfish and willingly yield to one another. Why? It is because the very survival of mankind may well depend upon our ability to build genuine interstate trust. Nowhere is the positive-sum nature of international relations more apparent than in the realm of the environment, a topic to which we will now turn.

On the Environment

When it comes to the issue of the environment, whatever direction China takes could irrevocably determine the future of mankind. For example, China is the world's biggest producer *and* importer of coal. While coal is abundant and cheap, it is also a dirty source of power which not only contributes to global warming (for the same amount of electricity generated, coal emits roughly twice as much carbon dioxide as natural gas) but also causes severe air pollution. Coal mining, too, is a problem: thousands of lives are lost in coal pit accidents each year[18] while waste from coal-washing and underwater leakage contaminate water and degrade soil.[19] Unfortunately, China currently depends on coal for over 80% of its electricity generation. Although the government has been actively promoting renewable and nuclear alternatives, coal consumption is expected to rise significantly in the medium term. Partly as a result, a recent study by McKinsey projects that China's emission of carbon dioxide will reach 15 billion tonnes by 2030 — more than twice its current level.[20]

The challenge may appear daunting, but then, to borrow a widely used cliché, the Chinese word for "crisis" represents both danger and opportunity.[21] Think of what we said earlier about the rise of China: if China were to truly replace the US as the global leader in the 21st century, China would need to become a model civilization for the world, a nation which addresses urgent problems facing mankind and offers hope for humanity. The US did not attain its status as the global leader simply because of its military power; rather, it led the world because of the real and genuine advances it achieved in science, business, and culture. Among others, it invented or made widely available the following: electricity, telephones, automobiles, airplanes, integrated circuits, computers, televisions, and the Internet. Culturally, it revolutionized the world of fashion with jeans and the casual look; music, with jazz and rock; cuisine, with fast food and soft drinks; and entertainment, with Hollywood movies and professionalized sports. Whatever one may think of the mass culture of the US, it is hard to deny that the American lifestyle mesmerized people around the globe with its allure — and represented a sort of universal living standard the rest of the world aspired to — for much of the past century. Sadly, though, the materialistic abundance of the US no longer inspires us as much as it used to, not only because other nations have caught up with it economically but also because the world has come to prefer something more diverse, humane, healthy, and ecologically sound.

China, then, has an opportunity to create a different kind of civilization, one which respects diversity, humaneness, health, and the environment, one which sets an example for the rest of the world. Concerning the environmental challenge in particular, there are reasons to believe that China is somewhat uniquely positioned to tackle it: the sheer size of its market, which allows the country to unilaterally dictate industry standards; its army of engineering and science graduates, growing by an estimated one *million* each year[22]; the single-party state which can take a longer-term view in policy planning and implementation than democratic states normally do; and the Confucian culture which emphasizes community and inner morality. With these factors in mind, let us now delve into China's environmental strategy. Here we have identified three key principles, namely that China should (1) actively manage the environment, (2) leverage capitalism, and (3) redesign our civilization.

1. Actively manage the environment

As we think afresh the concept of ecology, a good place to start would be to recognize that humans have a fundamental role in managing our ecosystem. Observe, for example, the following passage from the *Doctrine of the Mean*:

> It is only he who possesses the most complete sincerity who can fully realize his nature. Able to fully realize his own nature, he can do the same to the nature of other men. Able to give its full development to the nature of other men, he can give their full development to the natures of creatures. Able to give their full development to the natures of creatures and things, he can assist Heaven and Earth in their transforming and nourishing powers. Able to assist their transforming and nourishing powers, he may form a trinity with Heaven and Earth.[23]

The progression to sagehood begins by possessing the utmost sincerity, which is seen as the key to self-realization. It then proceeds to transforming other men, followed by helping the development of animals and things, and culminates in forming a "trinity" with Heaven and Earth. What is a trinity? The Trinity in Christianity refers to the Father, the Son, and the Holy Spirit, which are distinct and yet the same, meaning they are different manifestations of one God. Of course, the Confucian trinity of Heaven, Earth, and Man does not carry such a religious undertone; it is simply an expression of the Confucian worldview that Heaven, Earth, and Man are the three key partners in our biosphere who jointly nourish and cultivate all living beings. Heaven is a kind of *yang* which provides sunlight and rain; Earth represents *yin*, a womb from which all creatures draw their nutrition; and Man, who embodies both *yin* and *yang*, is responsible for ordering and managing all living beings and their relationships. In short, the defining characteristic of Confucian cosmology is the remarkable importance it assigns to the human species. That is why Zisi describes the role of a sage as not just transforming human society but caring for the natural world as well.

In contrast, Taoists bristled at the suggestion that humans should play (in a manner of speaking) the role of God. Is it not hubris for humans to assume that they are equal partners with Heaven and Earth, or to even contemplate that they can improve upon the workings of nature? Instead, Taoists argued that men should leave Mother Nature alone, in accordance with their "let it be" philosophy. Because "naturalness" was central to Taoism, it exhibited anti-civilization tendencies, and its adherents often led simple and rustic lives away from the hustle and bustle of big cities. Living in harmony with nature, rather than manipulating it, was held up as the ideal.

As it happens, Taoism is much closer to the position of modern environmental movements than Confucianism. Most environmentalists also advocate minimizing human influence on the environment. Their philosophy is reflected in the vocabulary they employ: we need to "conserve" nature by reducing our ecological "footprint." By way of illustration, the genetic engineering of crops, which "meddles" with biological processes, is seen as a bad thing, although farmers and animal herders have practiced selective breeding safely for thousands of years. The problem with this view is that it calls into question the very idea of progress, on the assumption that industrial growth inevitably leads to resource depletion and environmental degradation. In fact, if we push this line of thinking to its logical extreme, we arrive at the depressing conclusion that human civilization itself is a sin. Think of Rousseau's famous opening line in *Émile*: "Everything is good as it leaves the hands of the Author of things; everything degenerates in the hands of man." If this philosophy is correct, we might as well go back to living in caves, without electricity or flushing toilets — or better yet, sterilize ourselves.

While most environmentalists will not go that far, a lighter version of this view can be seen in the following counsel by James Lovelock, proponent of the Gaia hypothesis:

> For longer-distance travel, to ease that peripatetic itch we all seem to have, we could use sailing ships again... It would take longer than a jet but, as is often said, it is usually better to travel than to arrive.[24]

Here, Lovelock recommends that we should do away with air travel altogether in order to reduce carbon dioxide emission. He then goes on to attack the Christian notion of "stewardship of nature," arguing that it is "flawed by unconscious hubris," and sarcastically adds that "we are no more qualified to be the stewards or developers of the Earth than are goats to be gardeners".[25]

Which view is correct? While we acknowledge and accept the wisdom of respecting the natural state of things as much as possible, we still prefer the humanist conception of sustainable development which is implicit in the Confucian view, for the following reasons: first, we cannot just go "back to nature" as Rousseau suggests, however romantic the idea may sound. As Confucius once retorted to a Taoist recluse, "It is impossible to associate with birds and beasts, as if they were the same with us. If I associate not with these people — with mankind — with whom shall I associate?"[26] We are firmly and irrevocably within human civilization, a fact we might as well recognize, along with the responsibility it entails. Second, it is an illusion to assume that we have any viable alternative to economic growth. As Mark Lynas points out in *The God Species*, "The alternative to growth in the modern market system is painful contraction, unemployment, and political instability".[27] Besides, it would be morally wrong to deny poorer countries the opportunity to grow their way out of poverty. Third, and most important, we *can* redesign our civilization in such a way that our progress is not just less harmful but neutral or even beneficial to the environment, as we shall see shortly. Trees grow themselves while providing valuable services for their habitat. Why can't, say, our buildings do the same?[28]

The truth is that we are already playing the role of God, whether we admit it or not. Icecaps in Greenland are melting because of our industries. The Fukushima earthquake may have been a natural disaster, but its consequences would not have been nearly as bad without the manmade nuclear catastrophe. It is time to acknowledge the awesome power we have in our hands and to accept the great responsibility which accompanies it.

2. Leverage capitalism

Capitalism and ecology do not have to be at loggerheads with each other. We have already mentioned that an Asian developmental state harnesses the vibrant private sector to advance its social development goals; the same approach can be applied to solve the energy-climate challenge as well.

The defining characteristic of the energy-climate challenge is its global scale. Trying to address it at the individual level can sometimes feel like (to borrow a timeworn but appropriate cliché) rearranging the deck chairs on the *Titanic*. One can recycle plastic bottles, ride a bike to work, change light bulbs, and use reusable bags for shopping. These are all great habits, to be sure. However, such well-intentioned efforts by individuals and households may well shrink to irrelevance, unless we put a halt to the inexorable rise of coal-based power across Asia, from China to the Philippines to Indonesia to Bangladesh to India. As Thomas Friedman bluntly puts it, "[T]he energy-climate challenge we face today is a huge scale problem. Without scale, all you have is a green hobby".[29]

When it comes to clean energy, the deployment of technology matters as much as its development. The cleanest technology in the world will not make any difference to the climate change unless we deploy it *en masse*, on a scale that matters from a planetary point of view. Unfortunately, while we have many venture capitalists in Silicon Valley financing the latest advance in clean technology, we do not have nearly enough investors financing renewable energy projects in the fast-expanding economies of Asia. And this is the crux of the problem. Emissions in the European Union and the US have

already peaked, and will keep falling; the real fight is in the power
sector of emerging markets. As Mohamed Nasheed, former president
of the Maldives, observes, "What developing countries choose, in
particular whether they power their growth with coal or clean energy,
will dictate whether or not humanity can avert a climate catastrophe".[30] Given the situation, it is a pity that a country like Indonesia,
with a population of 240 million, still does not have a single utility-
scale solar power plant, although it is a tropical nation with plenty
of sunshine.[31] (As a sidenote, back in 2008, Jung-kyu tried to put
together a clean technology fund with a mandate from the
Government Investment Unit of Indonesia, but the public–private
partnership was aborted due to the global financial crisis.)

In comparison, the Chinese government has generally been
superb in its promotion of renewable energy. China is the largest
producer of wind power in the world, with installed capacity of 62
GW as of 2011.[32] The country lags behind the US in solar power
generation, but it is catching up fast; according to one estimate, it
will have 35 GW of photovoltaic-based capacity by 2016.[33] Solar
water heating is implemented extensively in buildings across
China, from the new terminal in Beijing airport to a village inn in
Yunnan province.[34] The success of wind and solar projects in China
is an example of state-directed capitalism at its finest, whereby private developers leverage the support of municipalities to secure
cheap debt financing and sign long-term power purchase agreements. Partly as a result, China is now the world's leading manufacturer of wind turbines and solar modules, and it has been
investing heavily in electric vehicles and minimum-impact public
transportation as well.

This is not to deny that China still has major challenges ahead.
Even with the rapid scale-up in renewable energy, the current five-
year plan pledges China to meeting only 11.4% of its energy demand
from non-fossil fuels (including hydropower) by 2015.[35] Further
reforms are certainly required, including drastic changes in energy
pricing and the introduction of emissions trading and/or carbon
taxation.[36] All the same, China's accomplishments hold a lesson for
the rest of the world, namely that social goals such as tackling global

warming can best be achieved by the state and the private sector working together.

What drives private investors is, of course, return. As long as the return expectation is high, money continues to pour in. Think of all the property developments in Dubai or Shanghai circa 2007, when almost half of the world's construction cranes were said to be operating in those two cities. The question is how to bring this kind of investment boom to the renewable energy sector in emerging markets, so that it may achieve the scale necessary to counter the resurgence of coal.

Which brings us to the role of financial services: the sector has been vilified for its short-sighted greed, but it has an opportunity to redeem itself (and also profit handsomely in the process) by addressing the challenge of financing renewable energy projects in developing nations. Right now, it is quite difficult to find equity investors for these types of projects, because the perceived "country risk" is high. At the same time, however, expected return on equity also tends to be high — usually in double digits, at least in terms of local currency — so the challenge should not be insurmountable. If our investment bankers and fund managers can come up with creative products which optimize the risk-return balance, then clean energy could present an ideal investment opportunity for long-term investors looking for stable high yields, with the added bonus that such investment will help save the planet. Innovation in finance got a bad name following the 2008 crash, but the whiz-kids on Wall Street can play a crucial, positive role in our quest for sustainable development, if only they choose to put their brilliant minds to it.

3. Redesign our civilization

William McDonough and Michael Braungart expounded the notion of cradle-to-cradle design in their groundbreaking book, *Cradle to Cradle: Redesigning the Way We Make Things*, in 2002. One may say their approach is biomimetic, in that they advocate redesigning our products and buildings as if they were regenerative living mechanisms. We cannot pursue all the details of their fascinating work here, but some of the general principles include the following:

- Products should be redesigned from scratch in such a way that they become essentially non-polluting and waste-free. Specifically, we need to ensure that the materials used in a product can be effectively separated into organic nutrients (biodegradable materials which can be disposed safely) and technical nutrients (minerals and synthetic materials which can be reused in continuous cycles without deterioration in their quality). No toxic material which is harmful to human health or the natural environment may be used, unless there is absolutely no alternative.
- Buildings should be designed around natural and cultural landscapes, taking advantage of natural sunlight and airflow to maximize energy efficiency, while being aesthetically unique and pleasing. Such buildings should also enhance the lives of the people who inhabit them, by providing a range of natural and cultural pleasures. Again, the building materials should be biodegradable or truly recyclable, and the use of harmful chemicals should be minimized or eliminated altogether.

Among the most potent imageries presented in the book are those of a cancer and a cherry tree. Environmentalists tend to see industrial growth as a cancer which "grows for its own sake and not for the sake of the organism it inhabits".[37] Who could disagree, seeing all the ugly urban sprawls which blanket the natural landscape under layers of asphalt and concrete? What McDonough and Braungart argue, however, is that things do not have to be this way. Think of a cherry tree, which not only seeks its own growth but also serves its habitat in a number of positive ways, including: providing food for animals and insects; cleaning air and water; creating and stabilizing soil; harboring a diverse array of flora and fauna; and returning to the soil when it dies, releasing nutrients which will fuel new growth. What this means, according to McDonough and Braungart, is that the tree is "not an isolated entity cut off from the systems around it… [but rather] inextricably and productively engaged with them".[38]

What makes the work of McDonough and Braungart so exciting is that they have been successfully implementing their vision through consulting assignments in one sector after another, with a range of clients that includes Ford Motor Company, Herman Miller, Nike, and SC Johnson. For instance, Nike is developing shoes which can do without the toxic process of leather tanning, along with a product take-back program to retrieve the uppers, outsoles, and cushioning midsoles — all of which are designed to be separable and completely recyclable.[39] According to the company website, Nike's Reuse-A-Shoe program has recovered over 23 million pairs of shoes to date. In another example, the factory which the authors designed for Herman Miller is characterized by abundant daylight, which diminishes the need for fluorescent lights; natural airflow, which cuts down the need for air conditioning; and connections to wetlands, which channel storm water and cleanse waste water.[40] Other bright ideas employed by the authors include "biological machines" which use hungry microorganisms to treat sewage effluents, and "green rooftops" covered with a layer of native grasses which absorb water runoff and provide habitat for many species, while protecting the building from thermal shock and ultraviolet degradation.[41]

Admittedly, redesigning products from scratch to achieve a zero-waste supply chain, or customizing buildings to take advantage of natural and cultural landscapes, is much more difficult and time-consuming than standard industrial design. For example, when McDonough and Braungart were commissioned to create a compostable upholstery fabric, they were turned down by 60 chemical companies before finally finding one European company willing to accept the challenge; with its help, they scrutinized almost 80,000 chemicals which are commonly used in the textile industry. The result justified the efforts, though, by removing the need for additives and corrective procedures. Later, regulators visiting the textile mill "thought their instruments were broken" because they could not identify any pollutants in its effluents — not even those which existed in the water entering the factory! [42]

To sum up, cradle-to-cradle design requires a far greater amount of resources (including all the engineering work) during the design and implementation stage, but additional costs are more than offset by energy savings and other benefits later on. Actually, this kind of challenge should excite the vast army of engineers in China. Necessity is the mother of all inventions, and when we reframe the challenge in a new fashion, it tends to bring forth creative solutions which have not been thought of before.

* * *

Ian Morris, in his magisterial work *Why The West Rules – for Now*, notes the remarkable technological advances China achieved during the Song dynasty (CE 960–1279). The Song period may be considered the golden age of Chinese civilization, with the greatest number of indigenous scientific and social innovations. Among the notable innovations were: paper money, which started as government-issued bills of credit and became the world's first banknotes in 1024; movable-type printing, invented centuries before Gutenberg, which churned out millions of books and drastically boosted the literacy rate; joint-stock companies, combined with the development of large oceangoing junks and the magnetic compass, which financed booming overseas trade (Song merchants were active in India, the Middle East, and Eastern Africa); the widespread use of coal, which not only warmed millions of homes, but also powered thousands of smelting furnaces for producing cast iron (cast iron was not introduced to Europe until the 14th century); a pedal-powered silk-reeling machine, which revolutionized textile production and quite possibly inspired Western designs later on; and gunpowder for use in warfare, which led to the invention of the gun-barrel and the projectile-fire cannon.[43]

Despite being labeled copycats, the Chinese are actually some of the most creative people in the world, as these Song-era innovations demonstrate. We hope they will take on the task of redesigning our civilization in a manner which is more humane, aesthetically pleasing, and sensitive to the environment — in other words, in accordance with *ren* — and produce the kind of trailblazing innovations which the US gave us so much of in the last century.

Celebrating China's Rise

Many Western observers regard the rise of China as a threat, not only because of what it means to the hegemonic status of the US in world politics, but also because of what they see as the ideological incompatibility of China with the value systems of the West. As Henry Kissinger, who pioneered a policy of *détente* with the Soviet Union and reopened the US–China relations, wryly observes:

> Neoconservatives and other activists would argue that democratic institutions are the prerequisite to relations of trust and confidence. Nondemocratic countries, in this view, are inherently precarious and prone to exercise of force. Therefore the United States is obliged to exercise its maximum influence... to bring about pluralistic institutions where they do not exist, and especially in countries [such as China] capable of threatening American security.[44]

According to the hawks in Washington, a clash between the US and China is inevitable as long as China stays undemocratic. To preempt this eventual crisis, the US must assist the Chinese in making a transition to democracy. The strategic objective of the US, in other words, is to bring about a regime change in China — an audacious goal, to say the least.

It is precisely the same argument the Neoconservatives have employed to justify the invasion of Iraq in 2003. Kissinger wisely scoffs at this view, arguing that an attempt to contain China for "an ideological crusade" would only strengthen the hands of the hawks in Beijing — any diplomatic pressure or economic sanction by a foreign power would be interpreted by the Chinese through the lens of nationalism — and the resulting escalation of tension would lead to "disaster for both sides".[45] It is far better to recognize that China and the US must cooperate as much as they compete, for three reasons. The first reason is economic. Unlike the former Soviet Union, China is a major trading partner for the US and the rest of the world. Prolonged confrontation between the two countries would have debilitating consequences for the global economy. The second reason is military and technological. In addition to their nuclear arsenals, both superpowers possess ultra-modern military technologies of unknowable consequences. Any serious conflict would almost surely devastate the victor as well as the vanquished. The third reason to advocate a harmonious relation is that the very survival of our civilization might hinge upon it. In the inter-connected world of the 21st century, the major powers have no more important responsibility than to take the lead in solving the urgent global problems facing mankind, including climate change, energy security, nuclear proliferation, epidemic diseases, migration, and food and water shortages. Since the Sino–US partnership in all likelihood represents the best hope of effectively tackling these challenges, it is imperative that both nations overcome their ideological differences and build genuine mutual trust.

Some scholars of international relations draw a parallel between the rise of China and those of Germany and Japan during the inter-war period, to show that a collision between the status quo power and a rising power is inevitable. But this is a totally inappropriate example to draw upon. A better parallel, in our view, is the rise of America during the 19th and early 20th century, which was not only tolerated but encouraged and celebrated by the very Europeans whose power was being eclipsed. How could this be? It was because America, the first country to embrace the principles of modern democracy, individual freedom, and universal human rights, represented a hope for humanity. Europeans, whose own progress was blocked by their monarchs and clergymen, desperately wanted the American experiment to succeed.

Can something similar happen in the 21st century? Can we envision a future in which the rest of the world cheers as China rediscovers its historical dominance and pre-eminence? It may all sound far-fetched, considering where China stands today. Externally, the country has been augmenting its military capability and asserting its sovereignty over Taiwan and the Spratly Islands. Territorial claims aside, pointing hundreds of short-range missiles at fellow Taiwanese and bullying its smaller neighbors in Southeast Asia hardly seem like a sign of magnanimous leadership. Internally, we are observing a stunning collapse of social values, as exemplified by corrupt bureaucrats and unethical merchants. The demise of communist ideals, combined with bold capitalist experiments, has resulted in a materialistic culture which is breathtaking in its cynicism.

What we have sought to demonstrate in this book, though, is that culture *can* be transformed by moral leadership — and, just as importantly, a clear social vision. We hope that China seizes the Confucian vision and realizes a society which can serve as an inspiration for the rest of the world, a society which overcomes the shortcomings of the American civilization and successfully addresses the multiple problems which modernity poses for humanity. If China becomes just another America (or even worse, three or four Americas combined), with its materialist values, military expansionism, and environmental degradation, then the world will have no reason to welcome its emergence. If, on the other hand, China becomes a model civilization for the world, achieving a healthy and prosperous society internally and projecting a magnanimous and intelligent leadership globally — in a way that America is currently failing to do — then the world will surely laud and embrace its rise.

A Short Introduction
to Confucianism

Benevolence is the most comfortable house of man, and righteousness is his only straight path. Alas for them, who leave the tranquil dwelling empty and do not reside in it, and who abandon the right path and do not pursue it?

Mencius, 4a-10

Confucius and Religion

Confucius was born in a religious environment. His father was a descendent of the Shang people, who were exceedingly zealous in their religious beliefs. What little we know about the Shang dynasty (1600–1046 BCE), which preceded the Zhou, comes from their religious relics: vast amounts of bronze ritual vessels and so-called "oracle bones." The latter mainly consist of turtle shells and bones, which turned out to be extremely valuable because of the inscriptions they contained. Oracle bones are China's oldest texts. Ian Morris, in his characteristically witty style, describes the fortune-telling rituals as follows:

> The king would put questions to his ancestors, summoning their spirits… Pressing a heated stick against a shell or bone, he would interpret the cracks it produced, and specialists would inscribe the results on the

"oracle bone"… The rites made [the king] ancestor-in-chief, hosting parties for spirits of recently dead kings… The rituals also involved binge drinking, perhaps to put the king and diviners into the right frame of mind for talking to spirits.[1]

Lots of drinking and orgies accompanied these rituals. The glittering court life of the late Shang period is captured in the proverbial expression "lakes of wine and forests of meat," where "naked men and women chased one another and drank long into the night".[2] The more sinister aspect of the Shang religion involved human sacrifices. Archaeologists excavated a tomb in Anyang, the last capital of Shang, containing about 200 corpses, some of whom were beheaded or had their limbs chopped off; the rest were bound and contorted, indicating they were buried alive. Approximately 5000 sacrificial pits have been identified around the tomb. It has been estimated that during the 150 years that Anyang served as Shang's capital, a quarter of a million people may have been sacrificed in this manner, mostly as appendages to the funerals for the elites.[3] Royals presumably required the service of hundreds of slaves in the afterlife.

Confucius was born in 551 BCE, almost five centuries after the fall of the Shang dynasty, but religious superstitions had survived in various parts of the society. We already mentioned that the father of Confucius was a descendant of Shang refugees. His mother came from a family of shamanic mediums who served as intermediaries between the dead and the living, and who also administered funeral rites. Sima Qian, the great historian who left the most authoritative biography of Confucius, includes this description of his childhood:

Confucius loved "playing house" when he was small. He would always set out on the table wooden blocks and plates used in funerals, and dress up in a way appropriate for ceremonies.[4]

As a child, Confucius was steeped in religious culture. Yet when he grew up, the Duke of Zhou became his hero. The Duke of Zhou was the brother of King Wu, who defeated the Shang dynasty in 1046 BCE. Because King Wu passed away only a couple of years after his victory, the Duke became the regent of his 13-year-old nephew who had succeeded King Wu. It was the Duke who consolidated the rule of the newly founded dynasty. We could say that the culture of Shang was a culture of the dead, as symbolized by its massive tombs, religious rites, and frequent intoxication. The Duke sought to instil a culture of the living instead, by replacing the "drunken" Dionysian culture of the Shang with a new, "sober" Apollonian culture. Just how greatly he detested the inebriation of the Shang court is evident in the *Classic of History*, in a section called "The Announcement about Drunkenness." He sought to dispel the religious madness of the Shang dynasty and introduce a more rational humanism in its place. To do so, he replaced Di, the highest god in Shang mythology, with a more abstract notion of the Mandate of Heaven, which meant something akin to the voice of people.

Confucius descended from the Shang diaspora, but he consciously shed his Shang heritage — just as Jesus shed his Judaic heritage — and identified himself as a subject of Lu, a vassal state where the Duke of Zhou had been enshrined. As the *Analects* quotes him, "How its culture shines! I will follow the Zhou".[5] Confucius saw it as his mission to uphold the humanist tradition as defined and passed down by the Duke. In another passage Confucius confesses, "I must be getting old. It has been so long since I met the Duke of Zhou in my dreams".[6] So the Duke must have frequently appeared in his dreams when he was young, just as a long-separated lover might appear in our dreams. In practice, negating the Shang and embracing the Zhou meant demystifying the religious ceremonies he had grown up with. Once Confucius took the shamanic impulses out of the ceremonies, what remained were rites and music. He preserved both, but principally as a means to civilize human society, rather than as a way to soothe spirits. He transformed religious rites into human rites. As his disciple Zheng Shen observed, even funerals and ancestor worships were held primarily for the spiritual benefit of the living, not the dead.[7]

It would be wrong to say that Confucius *denied* religion, though. He fully recognized that the need for the divine was an important part of human nature, and he allowed for the possibility that there were mysteries in the universe which one could never fully comprehend. It was just that the "here and now" mattered more to him. After the premature death of Yanhui, his favorite pupil, a disciple asked him about serving spirits. Confucius replied, "While you cannot serve the living properly, how can you serve spirits?" When the same disciple then asked about death, Confucius replied, "When you do not know enough about life, how can you know death?"[8]

When another disciple asked Confucius about knowledge (in ancient times the term could imply possessing intimate knowledge of the divine), Confucius replied:

> True knowledge is to exert one's efforts to duties of men and, while respecting the spirits, to keep a distance from them.[9]

Confucius did not bother to counter those who believed in the existence of spirits. What would be the point of arguing over the unknowable? He respected that some people had religious experiences while others didn't, and he left it at that. Rather, he tried to settle the question of religion by putting a proper distance between men and gods. We find this approach infinitely wiser than that of Nietzsche, who famously declared that "God is dead." Not only did Nietzsche fail to put God to rest, but he eventually went mad. The modern principle of separation of church and state also refers to the proper distance the government must keep from organized religions.

Another implication of Confucius's statement is this: those who are too close to the gods (the fanatics) would find it hard to acquire true knowledge because they tend to be stubborn and dogmatic in their beliefs. It is a trap into which many devout practitioners of religion fall — a stance which is not compatible with modern science. What distinguishes an advanced religion from a primitive religion, in our view, is the ability of an advanced religion to keep an open mind and accept criticism. By this criterion, modern Christianity would undoubtedly qualify as an advanced religion. Even the Vatican, which has long maintained the doctrine of papal infallibility, issued many retractions and apologies over the past half century, although bigotry and intolerance persist in extremist fringes.

The astonishingly modern view of religion held by Confucius did not arise out of thin air. Thousands of years before Max Weber spoke of rationalization, secularization and "disenchantment," the Zhou civilization went through its own version of demystification and demythologization. Let us illustrate this development with an episode concerning Zi Chan, prime minister of the state of Zheng. (Whenever we refer to a "state" in the Spring and Autumn period, it means a vassal state of the Zhou. Confucius was a native of the state of Lu, while Zigong was from the neighboring state of Wei. By the time of Confucius, the king of Zhou was reduced to irrelevance, and most vassals acted like independent lords.)

According to the *Spring and Autumn Annals*, a powerful shaman categorically declared in 523 BCE that a great fire would sweep over the state of Zheng. To save the country from the impending disaster, the people of Zheng scrambled to donate treasures to the gods and organize grand rites. The prediction came on the heels of several big fires in neighboring states, so the panic was understandable. Nevertheless, Zi Chan calmly reassured the people: "The Way of Heaven is far away, and the Way of Man is near. The Way of Heaven is, in fact, too far for us to fathom. How can [a shaman] claim to understand it?" No treasure was donated, no rite was performed, and of course, no fire broke out.

A similar episode features Ximen Bao, who was appointed provincial governor in the state of Wei. Upon arrival at his post, he gathered farmers to listen to their complaints. In the ensuing discussions, he learned of the practice of human sacrifice. A powerful priestess, three elders, and corrupt bureaucrats conspired to extract religious donations, and they also demanded that a young woman be plunged into a river, supposedly to placate the river god. Ximen went to attend the ritual, accompanied by soldiers. As soon as the sacrificial victim came forward, Ximen shook his head: "The girl doesn't look good enough. I will find a better replacement." He grabbed the priestess and said: "In order not to anger the river god, we should send someone who is closest to him." Upon his order, the priestess was thrown into the river. He looked around at the disciples of the priestess: "Your master is not coming back. Go search for her." Then he ordered them thrown into the river, too, followed by the three elders. Finally he turned to the trembling bureaucrats: "It is very strange that the elders are not coming back. Shall we dispatch the bureaucrats who collected donations?" The bureaucrats knelt down and begged for forgiveness.

Zi Chan was a great statesman who enacted the first written code of law in China's history. Ximen Bao went on to become court advisor to Marquis Wen of Wei, and he is credited with creating China's first large-scale irrigation system (obviously without worrying about what the river god might think of his efforts). Both were rationalists who sought to dispel superstition, as these anecdotes demonstrate. Zi Chan was a contemporary of Confucius, while Ximen Bao came a bit later (he studied under a disciple of Confucius). Confucius, then, was hardly alone in his suspicion of religion, but he probably had the most sophisticated understanding of human nature, including its religiosity, and promulgated a philosophy which could plausibly stand in for organized religion as a guiding principle of human society.

Confucianism as a Moral Philosophy

While Confucius respected religious sentiments as an essential part of human nature, he clearly did not believe in the existence of a personified god telling us what to do, or punishing us in the afterlife if we did not obey. So what was his source of inner morality? Confucius held that a man who possesses *ren* cannot help but be moral. That, in essence, is the Confucian theory of morality.

What is *ren*? While *ren* is commonly translated as "benevolence" or "humaneness," its original meaning was closer to "an ability to feel" or "sensibility." A Chinese-speaking reader might ask, "But how do we know that? Confucius never clearly defined the meaning of *ren*." One way is to look up the meaning of *bu-ren*, the negative form of *ren*: in Chinese medicine, *bu-ren* means numbness or paralysis, i.e. the absence of feeling. So we can infer that *ren* must have originally meant having feeling or sensibility. The analogy with Western languages is striking: sensibility in Greek is *aisthēsis*, the origin of the word *aesthet-ics*. The negative form of *aisthēsis* is *an-aisthēsis*, or anesthesia, which means loss of the senses and is also used as a medical term.

ren (ability to feel)	*bu-ren* (numbness, paralysis)
aesthetics (sensibility)	*anesthesia* (general or local insensibility)

How the word *ren* came to encompass other meanings such as benevolence and humaneness is easy to see, if one thinks of the English term *empathy*. The word originally came from the German *Einfühlung* (feeling into) and denotes a capacity to feel what others feel. It is analogous to *projection* or *perspective-taking* — the ability to imagine oneself in another's shoes. The term has become popular, and its meaning has expanded to include new connotations such as "sympathy," "compassion," and even "altruistic concern for others".[10] The implicit assumption here is that identifying with how others feel is closely linked to our beneficence to them.

Since *ren* is also a multifaceted term, we will lay out the concept using several definitions: compassion, aesthetic sensibility, and humaneness.

1. Compassion

A popular illustration of this aspect of *ren*, often cited by Confucian scholars, appears in the following observation of Mencius, arguably the most important Confucian philosopher besides Confucius himself:

> ...if men suddenly see a child about to fall into a well, they will without exception experience a feeling of alarm and distress. They will feel it, not because they think to gain the favor of the child's parents, nor in order to seek the praise of neighbors and friends, nor from a dislike of the reputa-tion they might get as having been unmoved by it. From this we may per-ceive that the feeling of commiseration [i.e. empathy] is essential to men.[11]

If we see a small girl about to be injured, our instinctive response is to cringe in fear and rush to help her. For Mencius, such compas-sionate sentiment, based on our sensitivity to others' pain, forms the basis of our morality. In the passage above, he repeatedly stresses that there is no utilitarian calculation of self-interest involved in the feeling, because his goal is to show that there is something intrinsically good about human nature.

Peter Singer, in *The Expanding Circle*, points out that the range of human compassion has historically expanded to include increasingly greater numbers of people.[12] The scope of our unselfish concern can be widened beyond our immediate relations, to the rest of our society, or even to those who live halfway around the world. Although we might not feel the same degree of empathy toward strangers as we do toward our own children, *ren*, when cultivated this way, could plausibly make us act with decency toward people of a different class, race, or nationality.

2. Aesthetic Sensibility

Compassion based on empathy is a worthy moral sentiment. But the concept of *ren* as envisioned by Confucius goes deeper. Mencius, born a century after the death of Confucius, was a moralizer who could only comprehend one aspect of *ren*. Confucius was anything but one-dimensional. He was a free spirit, a jazz artist — we mean it literally, as he was an accomplished musician who compiled the *Book of Songs* — who improvised at will. We get a glimpse of his understanding of *ren* in the following exchange:

> A disciple asked Confucius, "If one were to refrain from asserting one's superiority, boasting about oneself, remembering petty grievances, or acting in greed, would you say such person has *ren*?" Confucius replied, "All those are difficult to achieve, but I cannot tell from those qualities whether the person has *ren* or not."[13]

Here Confucius indicates that moral virtues, however desirable they may be, are not enough. One also needs to cultivate aesthetic sensibility, so that one may be able to handle subtle moral issues arising out of complex real-life situations. For Confucius, morality is not about blindly observing a rigid set of rules, but about being able to form appropriate value judgments based on one's (developed) emotional response to a specific circumstance.

Aesthetic sensibility, on its own, is neither moral nor immoral. But there is a sense in which a person who can truly *feel* also tends to be moral. It is because the ultimate source of our moral inclination is (if we accept Confucius's view) our aesthetic impulse. We may postulate that since we all desire beauty, we also pursue nobility in our conduct. Confucian teachings are not a set of commandments telling us what to do. Rather, they are an exhortation to strive for a higher standard in life by honing our sensibility and cultivating good habits. The drive for such self-improvement should be found within our nature, namely the universal human desire for aesthetic perfection. To live one's life in style, with one's head held high, is a *choice* any person can make. We can choose to make our lives as beautiful and as noble as we wish. And we might as well do our utmost to make this society of ours beautiful and noble, too. Neo-Confucians developed this line of thinking to assert that anyone can, given one's choice and efforts, realize the ideal of sagehood.

3. Humaneness

A reader might object that basing moral judgment on *ren* is dangerous, as it implies there is no such thing as an absolute standard of good and evil. What one person likes or dislikes may not be the same as what another likes or dislikes. Is this not precisely the kind of moral relativism we have been up against?

We concede that Confucianism does allow for a degree of moral relativism. Philosophically speaking, the Confucian position is that there is no such thing as a universal moral principle which is valid regardless of the context. Is lying always wrong? Kant says one should not lie to a murderer standing outside one's house, even if the murderer is trying to kill a friend who is hiding inside. This is obviously ridiculous, and it shows the limit of deriving moral principles purely from reason. The "objective" moral standard, from the Confucian viewpoint, consists in the shared emotional response — the shared moral *taste*, if you will — we have as a society.

Nonetheless, it is very different from moral nihilism, based as it is on the "humaneness" of our moral judgment. Let us demonstrate this point with a familiar example. In Nathaniel Hawthorne's *The*

Scarlet Letter, moral judgment according to scripture would unequivocally condemn Hester Prynne as the adulteress and Reverend Dimmesdale as the adulterer. Yet, by the time they mount the scaffold together toward the end of the novel, the townspeople have all but forgiven them for whatever sin they may have committed. Confucius would have approved. Below is a well-known exchange from the *Analects*:

> The Duke of Sheh informed Confucius, saying, "Among us there are those who are very straight in their conduct. If a father has stolen a sheep, the son will bear witness to the fact." Confucius replied, "In our part of the country, those who are straight are different. A father covers for his son, and the son covers for his father. Straightness is to be found in this."[14]

Here Confucius is teaching us to be human before we are moral. This example is obviously problematic from a societal standpoint, but it does give us a sense of how Confucianism manages to be situational (flexible) and moral at the same time. If we read the passage carefully, we can see there is a subtle difference between the way the Duke and Confucius interpret the term "straight." For the Duke, it simply means "morally upright." For Confucius, it refers to the natural emotion a father feels for his son (and vice versa), which comes "straight" from the heart. We forgive Hester and Dimmesdale because the depth of their love, and the sincerity of their atonement, touches our hearts. Such humane morality, however judgmental, is actually quite different from moral relativism ("there is no objective basis of good and evil") or moral nihilism ("nothing really matters").

* * *

The chief concern of Neo-Confucians, who revived Confucianism during the Song period, was how to restore some sense of moral certainty to the world. If all the extravagant rhetoric of Buddhism and Taoism could not solve simple social problems like bureaucratic corruption and youth crime, what was its social value? That was why Neo-Confucians decided to return to the basics, seeking to reinstate a moral order based on the Confucian teachings of self-cultivation and social realization. The real-world agenda of Zhu Xi, the grand master of Neo-Confucianism, was to ensure that civil servants, who were given wide-ranging discretion in the municipalities they governed, behave responsibly in their jobs. He sought to achieve that goal by seizing on the Confucian idea that there was something fundamentally good about human nature, which could be cultivated to produce exemplary leaders. Although the world has become exponentially more complicated since then, our task is similar. The challenge of modernity is also one of morality. How might we bring back some sense of moral certainty to the world, in this God-deprived age of moral relativism? This passionate call by Mencius offers a clue:

> Mencius said, "With those who do violence to themselves, it is impossible to have a meaningful conversation. With those who throw themselves away, it is impossible to do anything together. To disown in his conversation propriety and righteousness — this is what we mean by doing violence to oneself. To say that one is not able to dwell in benevolence or pursue the path of righteousness — this is what we mean by throwing oneself away. Benevolence is the most comfortable house of man, and righteousness is his only straight path. Alas for them, who leave the tranquil dwelling empty and do not reside in it, and who abandon the right path and do not pursue it?"[15]

Mencius urges us to dwell in benevolence (*ren*) and pursue righteousness (*yi*), as they are the keys to leading a meaningful and satisfactory life. Failure to do so is tantamount to hurting oneself. Whatever we do in our lives, let's not give in to despair and self-abandonment! We see here that for Confucians, morality is not about following a set of rigid rules based on God's decrees; rather, it involves the active choice of a virtuous life based on an enlightened understanding of human nature.

Confucianism versus Legalism

As we noted earlier, Mencius maintained that there was something intrinsically good about human nature. Specifically, he said that a "feeling of commiseration" (empathy) constituted the basis of *ren*.

Hsun Tzu, another great philosopher of the Warring States period, disagreed. Consider the following opening of a chapter titled "The Nature of Man is Ugly":

> The nature of man is ugly — his goodness is only acquired through training. The original nature of man today is to seek for gain. If this desire is followed, strife and rapacity results, and the spirit of courtesy dies... Therefore to give rein to man's original nature, to follow man's feelings, inevitably results in strife and rapacity... there is reversion to a state of violence.[16]

Since it is human nature to "seek for gain," giving free rein to it would result in "strife and rapacity." This view resembles that of Thomas Hobbes, who observed in *Leviathan* that human nature "maketh men invade for gain," and therefore the state of nature is one of *bellum omnium contra omnes* (war of every man against every man). Hobbes went on to advocate rule by an absolute sovereign, as only a strong central government was seen as capable of imposing law and order — thus liberating the masses from the state of nature, which he famously described as "solitary, poor, nasty, brutish, and short." Hsun Tzu's view was much more nuanced, as his emphasis was on the civilizing role played by education, but it was perhaps inevitable that the political philosophy of his followers would lean toward the authoritarian stance of Hobbes.

The most influential students of Hsun Tzu were Han Fei and Li Si. The former expounded the doctrine of Legalism, while the latter implemented it under the aegis of the First Emperor. Legend has it that Han Fei was recruited by the First Emperor (then king of the state of Qin) who was enamored with his philosophy, but Li Si, feeling threatened in his position, conspired to have Han Fei killed. Obviously, there was not much love between these two brilliant classmates. All the same, the policies Li Si carried out as prime minister of the First Emperor faithfully stuck to Han Fei's doctrine of Legalism.

Han Fei's thinking went like this: the Confucian ideal of rule by benevolence, desirable as it may sound, is hopeless in practice. How can a ruler judge legal matters based on ambiguous criteria like humaneness (*ren*)? However good his intentions might be, his rulings would be accused of being partial and subjective. Therefore, a ruler needs a more objective governing principle, which is a clearly defined set of laws. If the ruler metes out rewards and punishments strictly according to the letter of the law, his judgments will be seen as impartial and fair. The ruler applying the law does not have to feel guilty, and the person being punished will not bear any grudges. Why rely on such abstract notions as accepted morality or the goodwill of the people, when the law suffices to maintain the state in order?

Han Fei stressed the impersonal nature of law enforcement. As the great sinologist Joseph Needham notes, "The law should, so to speak, apply itself, and not require the constant interference of the ruler." There was to be no exception in applying the law, regardless of mitigating circumstances. One story quoted by Han Fei, concerning Prince Chao of the state of Han, is particularly revealing:

> The prince, having got drunk and fallen asleep, was exposed to cold, whereupon the crown-keeper put a coat over him. When he awoke, he asked who had covered him, and on being informed, punished the coat-keeper but put the crown-keeper to death [because] the transgression of the duties of an office was worse than mere negligence.[17]

It is all rather frightening, isn't it? Law enforcement was intentionally amoral — in fact, officials were chosen for their "ruthlessness" in applying the law — and the only "virtue" which counted was adherence to the law as laid out by the lawgiving prince. The law had to be designed on the assumption that human beings were selfish. For example, the punishment for soldiers who ran away from battle had to be made worse than dying at the hands of an enemy. Rewards were also strictly performance-based, e.g. military rank depended on the number of enemies slain. The state of Qin was notorious for its severe rules and draconian punishments, which contributed greatly to its military success and eventually brought about the unification of China.

Nevertheless, the Qin dynasty fell apart after only 14 years. Every subsequent dynasty which followed the Qin consciously abandoned

Legalism and embraced Confucianism. Why? We find a clue in the following passage of the *Analects*:

> If people are led by laws, and order maintained by punishments, they will only try to avoid the punishment, with no sense of shame. If people are led by virtue, and order maintained by the rules of propriety, they will have the sense of shame, and moreover will have principles.[18]

Here Confucius is saying that inner morality, which he calls "the sense of shame," matters. If a ruler leads only with rewards and punishments (assuming the worst about human nature), then people will merely try to avoid breaking the law, with no sense of right or wrong. If, on the other hand, a ruler leads by high-minded principles (appealing to the better angels of our nature), then people will behave quite decently on their own.

Ultimately, it is the collective goodness of citizens which holds a society together, not the written statutes. What happened during the final days of the Qin dynasty is clear: as soon as the leadership began showing cracks, generals and local officials were all too ready to defect, as their obedience was built not on any real allegiance to the regime, but on fear of punishment. The glorious empire of Qin, which had produced the Great Wall and the Terracotta army, crumbled like a sand castle. The Qin dynasty is admittedly an extreme example, but it should warn us of the dangers of a purely incentive-based system which is agnostic of the moral character of its participants.

Failures of Confucianism

No introduction to Confucianism would be complete without discussing where Confucianism went wrong historically, and why. It starts with the problematic notion of filial piety, which has long been regarded as the supreme virtue in Chinese culture.

As adults we tend to forget, but love for one's parents is the primal emotion of a human being. Freud claimed infantile sexual experiences formed the basis of later psychological development. In contrast, Confucius regarded the attachment to one's parents as the foundation of emotional growth. In a controversial Japanese TV drama called *Mother* (2009), the heroine, who has decided to "abduct" a horribly abused child and become her surrogate mother, makes this insightful observation: "We all say a mother's love is the most unconditional love of all. But the truly unconditional love is the love a child gives to one's parents." A child does not care whether his parents are nice or mean, rich or poor, handsome or ugly. The child is always eager to please them and desires nothing in the world more than being loved back.

Parental love is just as deep. Here is another moving line from *Mother*: "Happiness is when you could love someone like your own life." Only a parent could say that. When a young man asks Confucius about filial piety, he replies, "Parents only worry over a child's illness".[19] Anybody who has raised a child will sympathize with this sentiment. When a child is healthy, parenthood is filled with rosy happiness. But when a child becomes seriously ill, the whole world turns dark with despair. Parents cast aside everything else and devote themselves to the child's recovery. When parents tell their children "Just stay healthy," they mean it literally and sincerely.

Given the above, it was only natural that Confucius regarded filial piety as the quintessential expression of *ren* and promoted the virtue of caring for one's parents. Confucius held that individuals who treated their parents with proper respect and care would also behave responsibly in society, and no doubt there is some truth to it. What he did not teach, however, was blind obedience. Note the following passage from the *Analects*:

> Lord Meng asked about filial piety. Confucius replied, "Don't contradict." On his way back, Confucius told Fanxu [a disciple who doubled as his carriage driver], "Meng asked me about filial piety, but I just said 'Don't contradict.'" Fanxu asked, "What did you mean by that?" Confucius replied, "It means to serve one's parents with manners when they are alive, and to bury and commemorate them with manners when they pass away."[20]

The dynamism of this short exchange is hard to convey, but let us try: Meng was one of the three powerful lords in the state of Lu. When Confucius was called in to give him counsel, he saw little choice but to oblige, but the old sage was not pleased to be ordered around in such a manner. So when Meng asked him about filial piety, he replied curtly: "Don't contradict." Then, on his way back, he began to feel uneasy. Undoubtedly Meng would have understood his answer in the conventional sense, as in "Don't disobey your parents." But filial piety surely cannot mean blind obedience. If a father teaches his son to steal, should the son obey and become a thief? Suddenly Confucius realized the need to redefine his words.

When your parents' order goes against your values, you can and should disagree. But there is an important caveat: even when you disagree, you should do so with manners. Many young people are confused about this point, but you don't have to be rude to your parents to assert your opinion. Here Confucius is teaching us that the key attribute of filial piety is not blind obedience but being respectful. Another passage makes this point clearer: "In serving your parents, you have to advise them delicately. Even if they don't follow your advice, respect them and do not contradict. Even when it is painful to do so, you should not be angry with them".[21] When you clash with your parents on an important matter, arguing logically often leads nowhere, as the differences are likely emotional rather than rational. The better way is to resolve it gradually, by showing respect and giving it time.

Unfortunately, such subtle nuances were all but lost on the followers of Confucius. Filial piety increasingly became a repressive set of protocols governing social behavior. Unquestioning obedience to elders, especially one's father, was upheld as a supreme virtue and enshrined in law. See, for example, the following legal discussion from a Qin period document (around 217 BCE), excavated from a tomb in Yunmeng county, Hubei province:

> Suppose a retired old man comes to the court, accusing his son of not being filial, and requesting the death penalty. Normally the death penalty requires three careful deliberations. Should this case be deliberated three times? That will be unnecessary. Execute the son right away, so that no such behaviour may ever escape punishment.

This is a terrible law. Nevertheless, such legal tradition survived in China throughout history. Even if a father killed his child, the court would not consider it a crime. The authority of the father became so absolute that a father no longer inspired love and respect, but rather instilled fear and submission. Rewards were given to so-called filial children, and memorials were built in their honor. Those who were labeled "unfilial," on the other hand, were ostracized and often dealt extreme punishments. This line of thinking originated from the *Classic of Filial Piety*, which states: "There are three thousand offences against which the five punishments are directed, and there is not one of them greater than being unfilial".[22]

The *Classic of Filial Piety*, although it is attributed to a conversation between Confucius and his disciple Zheng Shen, was most probably created by an unknown author in the third century BCE, toward the end of the Warring States period. It has dominated Chinese society ever since. The book was the first to be canonized among the Thirteen Classics of Confucianism. In some ways, it was even more influential than the *Analects*. Various rulers, ranging from Emperor Xuanzong of the Tang to Emperor Kangxi of the Qing, have annotated and promulgated it. Why?

The Warring States period, as the name implies, was characterized by bloody wars of conquest. Intellectuals began yearning for a powerful emperor who would bring peace to China, just as Machiavelli dreamed of a prince who would unite Italy in the 16th century. It was this vision of an orderly empire which propelled the unnamed author to pen the *Classic of Filial Piety*. The defining feature of the book is the parallel the author draws between obedience to the father and loyalty to the ruler: "As common men serve their fathers, so they serve their rulers, and they revere them equally".[23] By equating natural respect for one's father with reverence to the ruler, the author sought to give an emotional foundation to the imperial rule.

What underlay both loyalty and filial piety (as construed by the author) was a strong sense of vertical hierarchy, as the chapter structure of the book demonstrates.

Chapter 1	The Scope and Meaning of the Treatise
Chapter 2	Filial Piety in the Son of Heaven [i.e. emperor]
Chapter 3	Filial Piety in the Princes of States
Chapter 4	Filial Piety in High Ministers and Great Officers
Chapter 5	Filial Piety in Inferior Officers
Chapter 6	Filial Piety in Common People

This vision of social hierarchy turned out to be all too convenient for subsequent rulers. Just as sons obeyed their fathers, common men were to obey officers, who in turn took orders from their ministers, and so on, until it culminated in the Son of Heaven. Confucius would never have dreamed that the filial piety of an emperor should be any different from that of common men. Yet his philosophy had somehow been used to justify the absolutist rule of an emperor from the Han dynasty onward, in the same manner that the teachings of Jesus were distorted to legitimize the authority of Roman emperors, and subsequently, the Vatican.

Just as Christianity should go back to the original teachings of Jesus, Confucianism must also rediscover the non-hierarchical, non-authoritarian spirit of Confucius. If you read the *Analects*, you see that Confucius was the most unassuming man there ever was, who often highlighted his own failings to encourage his followers. There was not a hint of authority about him.[24] He readily admitted mistakes.[25] He treated a blind music teacher with just as much courtesy as he would accord a prince.[26] Nor did he submit to undue authority in others. Although he was of humble origin, he never flinched from challenging the most powerful men of his time.[27] As Hsun Tzu memorably puts it, "To follow the Way, not the king; to follow Righteousness, not the father; this is called the great conduct of man".[28]

During the last century, it was fashionable to blame Confucianism for various ills of pre-modern China: familism, authoritarianism, passivity, submission, and stagnation. Our discussion here serves to show that the charges were not entirely unfounded. In recent years the Chinese government has established hundreds of "Confucian Institutes" worldwide and Korea has also seen the revival of private Confucian academies, known as *seowon*. We see them as a broadly positive trend, but we also worry about the potential of such movements to condone reactionary values such as rigid hierarchy and unquestioning obedience. Those of us in the East need to ask ourselves: Do we really want to go back to the days when seniors could beat up their juniors with impunity, a practice which used to be common in our schools and barracks? Or bring back a society where our "rulers" would look down upon citizens as their "subjects"? We must not romanticize the past but rather acknowledge the real and great benefits which modernization has brought. Only then can we bring Confucianism back to life, so that it may once again become a force for human progress.

About the Authors

Young-oak Kim is widely considered the leading public intellectual in Korea. He is the bestselling social science author of all time in Korea, having sold over 2.5 million copies of his books to date. A series of his lectures on Confucianism, Taoism, and Buddhism have aired on national networks and garnered unprecedented ratings. The Chinese classics he translated into modern Korean are used as the most authoritative texts by young Koreans. He received a Bachelor's degree from the Department of Philosophy, Korea University, where he later served as a tenured professor. He received advanced degrees from the National Taiwan University, the University of Tokyo, and Harvard University. He currently serves as the inaugural chaired professor of Korean Studies at Hanshin University, a position established with donations by three municipal governments in Korea.

Jung-kyu Kim serves as director of ACA Investments, a private equity firm headquartered in Singapore. He has advised investments in various sectors including clean technology, media, IT, and healthcare, and chaired and spoken at several regional private equity conferences. He started his career at the Tokyo office of McKinsey & Company as a management consultant. He received a B.A. in Government from Harvard University and an MBA from INSEAD.

Endnotes

Preface

1. *Book of Rites*, Chapter 7.
2. *Ibid.*
3. The original source of this remark is Wallace Stanley Sayre. See Wikipedia, http://en.wikipedia.org/wiki/Sayre's_law.
4. *Analects*, 5-12.
5. See, for example, *Analects*, 12-7, 1-15, 12-23.
6. Brooks, D (2012). "How to Fight the Man," *The New York Times*, February 2.

Chapter 1

1. King, S (2011). *11/22/63*, Hodder & Stoughton, London, p. 712.
2. *The Economist* (2012). "Lyndon Johnson: That day that changed everything," May 5.
3. President Johnson's speech at the University of Michigan, May 22, 1964, LBJ Presidential Library. Available at: http://lbjlibrary.org/.
4. Available at: http://en.wikipedia.org/wiki/Great_Society.
5. See, for example, the comparison of Gini Coefficient between 1967 and 2005 in *US Census Bureau, 2004/06*.
6. Smith, E and Stark, C (2012). "By the numbers: Health insurance," *CNN.com*, June 28.
7. Ariely, D (2012). *The (Honest) Truth about Dishonesty*, HarperCollins, London, p. 27.
8. Polt, R (2012). "Anything But Human," *The New York Times*, August 5.
9. Cohen, R (2012) "Freer — and Less Free," *The New York Times*, August 2.
10. *Analects.*, 12-13.

11. Bell, D (2008). *China's New Confucianism*, Princeton University Press, New Jersey, p. 14.
12. Ramzy, A and Yang, L (2008). "Tainted-Baby-Milk Scandal in China," *TIME*, September 16.
13. *The Economist* (2005). "Obituary: Arthur Miller," February 17.
14. Chang, H-J (2010). *23 Things They Don't Tell You about Capitalism*, Allen Lane, London, p. 41.
15. Diamond, J (2012). "Romney Hasn't Done His Homework," *The New York Times*, August 1.
16. *The Economist* (2008). "Japanese finance: My bow is my bond," April 24.
17. Fukuyama, F (1995). *Trust: The Social Virtues and the Creation of Prosperity*, New York: Free Press, p. 351.
18. Barry, D (1998). "So many mysteries... so few clean clothes," *CNN/SI*, February 22.
19. Vecsey, G (1998). "Sports of the Times; A Verbal Gold Medal to a Perfect Host Nation," *The New York Times*, February 23.
20. Murray, C (2012). *Coming Apart: The State of White America, 1960–2010*, The Crown Publishing Group, New York, pp. 6–7.
21. See, for example, comments on the "culture war" by Pat Buchanan.
22. McGinn, C (2012). "Philosophy by Another Name," *The New York Times*, March 4.
23. Chomsky, N (2012). *Making the Future*, Hamish Hamilton, London, p. 236.
24. *Ibid.*, p. 238. The original quote is by Fritz Stern, an authority on the Nazi era and the Holocaust.
25. Schuman, M (2010) *The Miracle: The Epic Story of Asia's Quest for Wealth*, Harper Business, New York, pp. 149–150.
26. Kitto, M (2012). "You'll never be Chinese," *Prospect Magazine*, August 8.
27. Paraphrased from Brooks, D (2012). "How to Fight the Man," *The New York Times*, February 2.

Chapter 2

1. Quoted from Platt, S (2012). "Is China Ripe for a Revolution?" *The New York Times*, February 9.
2. Subramanian, A (2012). "The Great Currency Smackdown," *Newsweek Special Edition: Issues 2012*, p. 34.
3. Friedman, T and Mandelbaum, M (2011). *That Used to Be Us: How America Fell Behind in the World It Invented and How We Can Come Back*, Farrar, Strauss, and Giroux, New York, pp. 265–266.
4. Sachs, J. (2011). *The Price of Civilization: Economics and Ethics after the Fall*, The Bodley Head, London, pp. 116–126.

5. *People's Daily Online* (2007). "China's Central Party School trains 50,000 officials in 30 years," October 3.
6. Liu, M (2012). "Xi Jinping, China's Next President," *Newsweek*, February 6.
7. *Ibid.*
8. *The Economist* (2012). "Unrest in China: a dangerous year", January 28.
9. Available at: http://cpi.transparency.org/cpi2011/results/.
10. McGregor, R (2011). *The Party: The Secret World of China's Communist Rulers,* Penguin Books, London, p. 138
11. *Ibid.*, p. 139
12. *Ibid.*, p. 168
13. *Ibid.*, p. 94
14. Wines, M and Wong, E (2012). "In Charged Moment, China's Political Heir Tries Introducing Himself to U.S.," *The New York Times*, February 11.
15. Available at: http://www.novelguide.com/Bonfire-of-the-Vanities/toptenquotes. html.
16. McGregor, p. 99.
17. *Ibid.*, p. 141.
18. Federalist No. 51.
19. Benkler, Y (2011). *The Penguin and the Leviathan: How Cooperation Triumphs over Self-Interest,* Crown Business, New York, p. 197.
20. Sandel, M (2009). *Justice: What's the Right Thing to Do?* Penguin Books, New York, p. 193.
21. Benkler, p. 177.
22. *Ibid.*, p. 177.
23. *Ibid.*, p. 176.
24. Chang, p. 48.
25. Benkler, p. 197.
26. Sandel, p. 194.
27. *Analects*, 12-17, 12-18.
28. McGregor, p. 97.
29. *FoxNews.com* (2012). "Battle of the Billionaires — Super PACs Offer Chance for High Rollers to Sway 2012 Race," February 11.
30. *Analects*, 12-19.
31. *Ibid.*, 4-13.
32. Friedman and Mandelbaum, p. 243.
33. Kristof, N (2012). "Born Not to Get Bullied," *The New York Times*, February 29.
34. Benkler, p. 60.
35. Sachs, p. 80.
36. *Analects*, 12-7.
37. *The Economist* (2011). "Russia's Presidency: Guess Who!" October 1.
38. Krugman, P (2011). "The Post-Truth Campaign," *The New York Times*, December 22.
39. Available at: http://en.wikipedia.org/wiki/John_McCain.

40. Wine, M and LaFreniere, S (2011). "In Baring Facts of Train Crash, Blogs Erode China Censorship," *The New York Times*, July 28.
41. The University of Hong Kong (2011). "History of high-speed propaganda tells all," *China Media Project*, July 25.
42. The Economist "This year's model: A country on a roll, or rather a wave". Feb 18th 2012.
43. Sachs, p. 129.
44. *The Economist* (2012). "The future of the BBC: Auntie's big year," January 14
45. *Ibid.*
46. *The Economist* (2011). "Go East, young bureaucrat," March 17.
47. Kwang, HF *et al.* (2011). *Lee Kwan Yew: Hard Truths to Keep Singapore Going*, Straits Times Press, Singapore, p. 43.
48. Schuman, p. xxiv.
49. *Ibid.*, p. 32.
50. *Ibid.*, p. xxxiv.
51. Zakaria, F (1994). "A Conversation with Lee Kuan Yew," *Foreign Affairs*, March/ April, quoted from Schuman, p. 60
52. Schuman, p. xxxiii.
53. Available at: http://en.wikipedia.org/wiki/Lee_Kuan_Yew.
54. Schuman, p. 58.
55. *The Economist* (2011). "Go East, young bureaucrat," March 17.
56. Kwang, HF *et al.*, p. 101.
57. *Ibid.*, p. 124.
58. *Hsun Tzu*, 12-1.

Chapter 3

1. Needham, p. 35.
2. *Tao Te Ching*, Verse 17.
3. See, for example, Legge, J. *Sacred Books of the East*, Vol. 39.
4. *Tao Te Ching*, Verse 5.
5. Yu, H. *Study of the Way*.
6. Morris, I. (2011). *Why the West Rules — for Now: The Patterns of History and What They Reveal About the Future*, Profile Books, London, p. 381.
7. Yu, H.
8. *Mencius*, 1b-5.
9. *Ibid.*, 1a-7.
10. *Analects*, 6-28.
11. *Ibid.*, 6-28.
12. Hugo, V (1992). *Les Misérables*, Random House, New York, Preface.
13. Murray, C (2012). "Narrowing the New Class Divide," *The New York Times*, March 7.

14. Edsall, TB (2012). "Is This the End of Market Democracy?" *The New York Times*, February 19.
15. Warren, E and Tyagi AW (2004). *The Two-Income Trap*, Basic Books, New York, p. 5.
16. Warren, E (2007). "The Coming Collapse of the Middle Class: High Risks, Lower Rewards, and a Shrinking Safety Net." Part of the Jefferson Memorial Lectures series given at UC Berkeley on March 8.
17. Riley, C (2011). "25 hedge fund managers = $22 billion in pay," *CNNMoney*, April 1.
18. Bogle, J (2009). *Enough: True Measures of Money, Business, and Life*, John Wiley & Sons, Hoboken, NJ, p. 36.
19. Greg Smith, "Why I Am Leaving Goldman Sachs," *The New York Times*, March 14, 2012
20. See http://www.imdb.com/title/tt1615147/quotes
21. Bogle, p. 121
22. *Ibid.*, p. 214
23. Bernstein, J (2006). *All Together Now: Common Sense for a Fair Economy*, Berrett-Koehler Publishers, San Francisco, CA, p. 56.
24. *Ibid.*, p. 73.
25. Morris, I (2011). p. 504.
26. See http://www.goodreads.com/work/quotes/2792775-the-hunger-games.
27. Yasutomi, A (2011). *Ikiru tame no rongo*, Chikuma Shobo, Tokyo, pp. 208–209.
28. *Ibid.*, pp. 211–212.
29. Brooks, D (2012). *The Social Animal: The Hidden Sources of Love, Character, and Achievement* (New York: Random House, 2012), p. 281.
30. Available at: http://en.wikipedia.org/wiki/News_of_the_World_phone_hacking_affair.
31. Brooks, p. 316.
32. Smith, A *The Theory of Moral Sentiments*, Dover Publications, New York, p. 3.
33. Benkler, p. 187.
34. *Ibid.*, p. 188.
35. *Ibid.*, p. 189.
36. Fukuyama, p. 156.
37. *Mencius*, 1a-1, translation by Legge, used with modification.
38. Fukuyama, p. 156.
39. Benkler, p. 191.
40. Drucker, P (1954). *The Practice of Management*, HarperCollins Publishers, New York, p. 36.
41. *Great Learning*, Chapter 17.
42. Bogle, p. 203.
43. Bogdanich, W and Hooker, J (2007). "From China to Panama, a Trail of Poisoned Medicine," *The New York Times*, May 6.

44. *Ibid.*
45. *Ibid.*
46. Huang, Y (2012). "China's Corrupt Food Chain," *The New York Times*, August 17.
47. Hancock, T (2011). "Spate of Bridge Collapses Trouble Chinese Netizens," *Asiancorrespondent.com*, July 18.
48. Harney, A (2009). *The China Price: The True Cost of Chinese Competitive Advantage*, Penguin Books, London, p. 59.
49. *Ibid.*, p.65.
50. *Ibid.*, p. 57.
51. Based on a private interview.
52. Harney, p. 108.
53. *The Economist* (2012). "Consumers: Dipping into the Kitty," May 26.
54. Harney, p. 48.
55. *Ibid.*, p. 55.
56. Tselichtchev, I (2012). *China Versus the West*, John Wiley & Sons, Singapore, p. xix.
57. *The Economist* (2011). "Keynes vs Hayek in China," November 17.
58. Kristof, N (2012). "A Body, a Scandal and China," *The New York Times*, April 21.
59. *Ibid.*
60. Barboza, D (2012). "Billions in Hidden Riches for Family of Chinese Leader," *The New York Times*, October 25.
61. *Mencius*, 1b-5, translation by Legge, used with modification.
62. *Ibid.*, 1a-7.
63. *Ibid.*, 1a-7.
64. Benkler, p. 208.
65. http://en.wikipedia.org/wiki/NUMMI.
66. Benkler, p. 203.
67. *Ibid*, p. 211.
68. *Ibid.*, p. 210.
69. Wilkinson, R and Pickett, K (2010). *The Spirit Level: Why Greater Equality Makes Societies Stronger*, Bloomsbury Press, New York, pp. 183–184.
70. "Income distribution — Inequality: Income distribution — Inequality — Country tables," OECD Stats, 2012
71. *Mencius*, 3a-4.
72. Sandel, p. 18.
73. Sakamoto, K (2011). *Nihon de ichiban daiji-ni shitai kaisha*, Asa Publishing, Tokyo, p. 28, mobile edition.
74. Denning, S. (2011). "The Dumbest Idea In The World: Maximizing Shareholder Value," Forbes November 28.
75. *Analects*, 18-7.
76. Bogle, p. 200.
77. *Ibid.*, p. 201.

78. *Ibid.*, p. 202.
79. Brown, A (2010). *The Rise and Fall of Communism*, Vintage Books, London, p. 108.
80. McGregor, p. 30.
81. *Ibid.*, p. 606.
82. *Ibid.*, p. 11.
83. *Ibid.*, p. 12.
84. *Ibid.*, p. 14.
85. Russell, B (1945). *A History of Western Philosophy*, Simon & Schuster, New York, p. 364.
86. See, for example, *Mencius.*, 3a-4
87. Sandel, p. 220
88. *The Economist* blog (2011). "Elizabeth Warren: Liberal simplification," September 21.
89. *Analects*, 12-9.
90. *Mencius*, 1b-5.
91. Sachs, p. 227.

Chapter 4

1. *Mother Jones* (2004). "The Two Income Trap," November 8.
2. Quoted from Brooks, p. 196.
3. *Ibid.*, p. 312.
4. Chang, p. 188.
5. Murray, p. 47.
6. Brooks, p. 327.
7. Murray, p. 78.
8. *Ibid.*, p. 88.
9. *Ibid.*, p. 59.
10. *CNNMoney* (2011). "College costs climb, yet again," October 29.
11. Dewey, J (2004). *Democracy and Education*, Dover Publications, New York, p. 242.
12. *Ibid.*, p. 115.
13. Warren and Tyagi, pp. 33–46.
14. Chua, A (2011). *Battle Hymn of the Tiger Mother*, Penguin Group, New York, p. 259.
15. Abrahamson, E. (2012). "A Liberal Arts Education, Made in China," The New York Times, July 3.
16. Wong, E. (2012). "Test That Can Determine the Course of Life in China Gets a Closer Examination," The New York Times, June 30.
17. Yun M. and Lu, M. (2011). "Churchill's School Taps 'Nightmare' Hong Kong Waitlists for Bankers' Kids," Bloomberg.com, October 19.
18. *Ibid.*

19. Friedman and Mandelbaum, p. 100.
20. Chang, p. 178.
21. *Ibid.*, p. 181.
22. Friedman and Mandelbaum, p. 81.
23. *Mencius*, 6a-4.
24. *Ibid.*, 6a-10.
25. *Ibid.*, 6a-8, translation by Legge, used with modifications.
26. *Record on the Subject of Education*, Chapter 2.
27. Dewey, p. 109.
28. Whitehead, AN (1929). *The Aims of Education*, The Free Press, New York, 1929, p. 29.
29. *Ibid.*, p. 26.
30. *Ibid.*, p. 35.
31. *Analects*, 5-27.
32. *Ibid.*, 3-15.
33. *Ibid.*, 7-21.
34. *The Daily Mail* (2011). "Had a Row With Your Partner Today? That'll Be One of the 2,455 You Will Have This Year," 20 May.
35. Brooks, p. 22.
36. Bi, W. Annotation to *Tao Te Ching*, Chapter 38.
37. Kreider, T (2012). "Like the Video? I Wrote the Book," *The New York Times*, May 19.
38. Lieber, R (2012). "How to Raise a Financial Wizard," *The New York Times*, May 4.
39. *Hsun Tzu*, 2-8
40. Gladwell, M (2009). *Outliers: The Story of Success*, Little, Brown, and Company, New York, pp. 41–43.
41. *Ibid.*, p. 45.
42. *Doctrine of the Mean*, Chapter 9.
43. See, for example, *Analects* 6-5.
44. *Ibid.*, chapter 14, translation by Legge, used with modification.
45. Available at: http://www.cs.cmu.edu/~pausch/Randy/pauschlastlecturetranscript.pdf.
46. *Hsun Tzu*, 21-15.
47. *The Great Learning*, Chapter 11, translation by Legge.
48. Angle, S (2009). *Sagehood: The Contemporary Significance of Neo-Confucian Philosophy*, Oxford University Press, New York, p. 179.

Chapter 5

1. Fukuyama, F (2011). "The US Democracy has Little to Teach China," *The Financial Times*, January 17.
2. Krugman, P (2009). "The Big Zero," *The New York Times*, December 27.

3. Available at: http://data.worldbank.org/.
4. *The Economist* (2011). "Economics Focus: How to Get a Date," December 31.
5. Halper, S (2010). *The Beijing Consensus*, Basic Books, New York, pp. 9–10.
6. McGregor, p. 15.
7. *Ibid.*, p. 14.
8. Jacques, M (2012). *When China Rules the World*, Penguin Books, London, p. 534.
9. *Ibid.*, p. 613.
10. *Ibid.*, p. 250.
11. *Ibid.*, p. 19.
12. *Doctrine of the Mean*, Chapter 20.
13. Jacques, p. 594.
14. *Ibid.*, p. 595.
15. *Ibid.*, p. 594.
16. *Mencius*, 1a-3, translation by Legge.
17. *Tao Te Ching*, verse 61, translation by Legge, used with modification.
18. *BBC News* (2005). "China Orders Bosses Down Mines," November 7.
19. *The Economist* (2012). "Old King Coal," February 25.
20. *Ibid.*
21. Strictly speaking, this cliché is a misinterpretation of the term *weiji*.
22. *The Chronicle* (2011). "Number of US Engineers in Decline Relative to China, India," September 20.
23. *Doctrine of the Mean*, Chapter 22, translation by Legge, used with modification.
24. Lovelock, J (2007). *The Revenge of Gaia*, Penguin Books, London, pp. 170–171.
25. *Ibid.*, p. 176.
26. *Analects*, 18-6, translation by Legge.
27. Lynas, M (2011). *The God Species: How the Planet Can Survive the Age of Humans*, Fourth Estate, London, p. 240.
28. McDonough, W and Braungart, M (2002). *Cradle to Cradle: Remaking the Way We Make Things*, North Point Press, New York, p. 77.
29. Friedman, T (2007). "Save the Planet: Vote Smart," *The New York Times*, October 21.
30. Nasheed, M (2012). "Renewable Energy As Solution And Responsibility," *The Huffington Post*, August 24.
31. International Trade Administration, US Department of Commerce, *Renewable Energy Market Report: Indonesia*.
32. Available at: http://en.wikipedia.org/wiki/Wind_power_in_China.
33. The European Photovoltaic Industry Association.
34. Biello, D (2008). "China's Big Push for Renewable Energy," *Scientific American*, August 4.
35. Qiu, J (2011). "China unveils green targets," *Nature*, March 9.

36. *Ibid.*
37. McDonough and Braungart, p. 77.
38. *Ibid.*, p. 78.
39. *Ibid.*, pp. 181–182.
40. *Ibid.*, p. 75.
41. *Ibid.*, pp. 82–83.
42. *Ibid.*, p. 108.
43. Morris, pp. 377–383.
44. Kissinger, H (2012). *On China*, Penguin Books, London, p. 520.
45. *Ibid.*, pp. 524–526.

Bonus Chapter

1. Morris, p. 212.
2. Qian, S. *Records of the Grand Historian*, Annals of the Shang Dynasty.
3. Morris, p. 213.
4. Qian, S. *Genealogies*, House of Confucius.
5. *Analects*, 3-14.
6. *Ibid.*, 7-5.
7. See, for example, *Analects*, 1-9.
8. *Analects*, 11-11.
9. *Ibid.*, 6-20.
10. Pinker S. (2011). *The Better Angels of Our Nature: The Decline of Violence in History and Its Causes*, Allen Lane, London, p. 574.
11. *Mencius*, translation by Legge, Book 2, Part 1, Chapter 6.
12. Wright, p. 372.
13. *Analects*, 14-2.
14. *Ibid.*, 13-18.
15. *Mencius*, 4a-10.
16. *Hsun Tzu*, Chapter 23, translation based on the works of H. H. Dubs and Cheng Chih-I, quoted from Needham, pp. 19–20.
17. Needham, p. 207.
18. *Analects*, 2-3.
19 *Ibid.*, 2-6.
20. *Ibid.*, 2-5.
21. *Ibid.*, 4-18.
22. *The Hsiao King, or Classic of Filial Piety*, translation by Legge, Chapter 11.
23. *Ibid.*, Chapter 5.
24. See, for example, *Analects*, 3-15, 5-14, 7-23, and 9-6.
25. *Ibid.*, 7-30.
26. *Ibid.*, 15-41.
27. *Ibid.*, 12-17.
28. *Hsun Tzu*, 29-2.

Index